Maryland Wine

Maryland Wine

A FULL-BODIED HISTORY

Regina McCarthy

FOREWORD by KEVIN ATTICKS

THE
History
PRESS

Published by The History Press
Charleston, SC 29403
www.historypress.net

Copyright © 2012 by Regina Mc Carthy
All rights reserved

First published 2012

ISBN 978.1.60949.247.2

Library of Congress CIP data applied for.

Dedicated to my Jason, who often reminded me,
"The story is there. It is just waiting to be written."

And to Al Copp and Les Hubbard—my underpaid consultants, counselors,
agents, editors and constant cheerleaders. Thank you for believing in me.

Contents

Foreword

U nless you're from Maryland, it may be hard to believe that wine grows deep in the Old Line State. In fact, even Marylanders might be surprised that our local wine's history began in colonial times, its limits were pushed—and pushed right back—during Prohibition and our state is home to the author of the first book on winemaking in America, Philip Wagner.

Maryland's wine history struck me when I was touring vineyards in Sonoma County. A staffer in Kenwood Vineyard's tasting room—after hearing I was a Marylander—asked if I had heard of Boordy Vineyards. He explained that Kenwood sourced some of its vines from Boordy and used Philip Wagner's *American Wines and How to Make Them* as a guide early in the winery's development.

Upon my return to Maryland from the Sonoma trip, I launched an effort to visit all of Maryland's wineries—all ten. The personalities of the proprietors and their efforts to produce world-class wines convinced me to write a travel guide to the state's wine industry. But my research didn't even scratch the surface of Maryland's wine and grape history.

What you will find in this book is a detailed account of the early vineyard trials, the politics of the vine through Prohibition and into recent times and incredibly in-depth descriptions of the major personalities in our industry's history.

Regina McCarthy spent many hours driving around our region collecting documents that don't exist online, books that are long out of print and stories from individuals whose involvement in our industry are not known to recent entrants. She has gathered and cultivated stories by reuniting old friends and business partners and learned much from libraries and publication archives.

In addition to the formal documentation, Mc Carthy profiles the personalities of those who struggled to build a credible industry. Not everyone got along, but just about everyone worked together—setting aside deep philosophical differences—at critical moments to chart a positive course to further the industry.

The book traces the industry's pre-Prohibition existence and Marylanders' roles in Prohibition (and the sometimes antagonistic arguments against it), leading up to the creation of Maryland's first commercial winery, Boordy Vineyards, in 1945.

After Boordy's founding, Mc Carthy follows as the Aellens begin the build-out of what would become the Frederick Wine Trail with Linganore Winecellars at Berrywine Plantations. She examines the many wineries that would come and go before sturdy industry growth began in the mid-1980s through the early years of the next century.

Mc Carthy also highlights the major moments of the last ten years, including a conversation between grower Dick Penna and Senator Don Munson from Washington County that led to the formation of the Governor's Advisory Commission on Maryland Wine and Grape Growing, the Maryland Winery Modernization Act and, most recently, the passage of direct-to-consumer shipping.

The only downfall of *Maryland Wine: A Full-Bodied History* is that it is, by nature of it being a book—with a historical perspective, at that—unable to predict or report the lively future we look forward to experiencing with Maryland wine and locally grown grapes.

I hope readers appreciate Maryland's long history of wine growing while enjoying the latest vintage of the Free State's finest wines.

Kevin Atticks, DCD
Executive Director, Maryland Wineries Association

Preface

Write a book about the history of Maryland wine?" I asked. "Sure, I'll do it." Little did I know that in embarking on the journey of researching this project, I would learn about Maryland's own colonial vineyards, pre-Prohibition winemaking attempts, a "New Deal winery" and over fifty brave souls who make up the state grape and wine industry. I didn't realize I would meet the best friends, children and grandchildren of Maryland wine's founding fathers and be privy to stories told for decades but mostly unheard by the modern industry and larger Maryland wine community.

The history of the Maryland wine industry is deep, especially for what seems to be such a "new" industry. In the short time I have been working on this project, seven new wineries have opened in the state, and the development of new ventures shows no sign of slowing.

The stories you will read in this book start chronologically and conclude regionally. These stories are well known among some members of the industry but brand-new to most. Thankfully, the wine industry is one in which secrets are shared—whether about pruning vines, crushing grapes or selling wine—and I was greeted with open arms and many, many stories to include in this compilation.

In each of my interviews and conversations, one thing was consistent. These people—the new and the old—were and are venturing into brand-new territory. Each is doing something new or different and is carving a place for him- or herself. They are truly building an industry—building

A look at Sugarloaf Mountain Vineyards. *Courtesy of Sugarloaf Mountain Vineyard, photographer Richard Cress.*

a market, building a reputation, building on the foundation laid by the forefathers, the original vintage of Maryland wine.

In the year 2000, Maryland was home to only eleven wineries. Since then, an average of three to five wineries have opened each year. Today, wineries are planting twenty to sixty acres at a time, and experienced winemakers are looking toward Maryland from other parts of the country to explore this emerging region.

The quality of regional wine is doubling as fast as the numbers of acres being planted. More and more local wines win awards in international and national competitions and are gaining popularity in mainstream wine publications.

Part of the industry's success comes from the support of an active membership organization, called the Maryland Wineries Association (formerly the Association of Maryland Wineries). This nonprofit trade association and its board, made up of an owner from each winery in the state, set the tone and the pace for industry growth and development. The

Maryland Wineries Association's sister organization is the Maryland Grape Growers Association, or MGGA. MGGA is the organization in which grape growers—some commercial and some hobby—gather and discuss challenges and opportunities and to commiserate about life in the vineyard.

Maryland is home to major wine festivals, each bringing in twenty-five to thirty-five thousand wine drinkers a year, and its wineries are a vibrant part of Maryland's tourism, greeting visitors from in and out of state.

Most important are the "characters" of the industry—the grape growers, winemakers, winery owners, their staff and families and industry advocates. Each of these unique personalities makes up this diverse industry and should be celebrated.

Acknowledgements

This book would not have been completed without the shared knowledge, memories and efforts of:

Albert Copp and Laurie Schwartz
Leslie and Jean Hubbard
Rob and Julie Deford
Bill and Anne Kirby
Hudson Cattell
Linda McKenna
John McGrew
Kevin Atticks
Bob Lyon
Helle DiSimone
Claire Mowbray Golding and the
    Mowbray family
Lucie Morton
Jack and Lucille Aellen
Anthony Aellen
Eric Aellen
Lucia Simmons
Patrick Roddy
Karen Fedor

Bert and Lynne Basignani
Mike and Rose Fiore
Carol and Fred Wilson
Lois and Bill Loew
Charlie Daneri and Emily Williams
Warren Rich
Erik Bandzak
Ed Boyce and Sarah O'Herron
Tom Shelton
Mark and Kim Cascia
Al and Jennifer Cassinelli
Voytek and Alicja Fizyta
Kathryn Danko-Lord and Jack Lord
Tim and Sheryl Lewis
Ray Brasfield and Joyce
    Hongsermeier
Paul Roberts and Nadine Grabania
John Wilkerson and Denise
    McCloskey

ACKNOWLEDGEMENTS

the Tamminga family
Patty Power and Rob Miller
Harry Hepbron and Janel Griffith
Chris Kent
Chris Lang
Tien-Seng and Tara Chiu
the Cleary family
Diane Hale
Matt Cimino
Kevin and Teresa Mooney
Mary Beth and Dick Seibert
the Layton family
Ashby and Carrie Everhart
Peter and Mary Ianniello
Marzanna and Andrzej Wilk
Jan Luigard and Maura Cahill
the Southern Maryland Wine
    Growers Cooperative
John Behun and Mark Flemming

Joe and Jo-Ann Romano
Roy and Linda Albin
Mike and Barb Scarborough
Greg and Karen Lambrecht
Maggie O'Brien, Jim Grube and
    Tucker Grube-O'Brien
Ken, Ann and Melissa Korando
Mark Emon and the St. Michaels
    Winery team
the Sugarloaf Mountain Vineyard
    family
Morris and Janet Zwick
Doug and Maureen Heimbuch
Don and Judy Tilmon
Jennie Schmidt
Jack and Emily Johnston
Morgan Walters
the Grape Growers of Maryland

The following people deserve recognition for their support and guidance:

Jason Mc Carthy
Cathy and Ed Reilly
Rachel, Joe, Gina and Dominic Postorino
Richard, Renee, Ella and Colin Reilly
Rebecca, Steven, Carter and Reilly Malin
Mary, Tim, Siobhán and Sharon Mc Carthy and Sarah Kelly
Catherine Lang
Katie Logue
Caitlin Regan
Colleen Regan
Kara Regan
Danielle Allen
Maggie Frey
Jessica Oursler
Jade Ostner
Ashley Estill

Chapter 1

The First Mention of Wine and Grapes in Maryland

As Europeans settled in the Americas, there was a very clear and deliberate movement to plant grapes and make wine up and down the East Coast. The first attempts were made with either French varieties transported from Europe or from native wild grapes found in this new land. The very first mention of winemaking and grape growing in the United States was in the 1560s by the French Huguenots, quickly followed by the Jamestown settlers in the very early 1600s.

The first mention of winemaking in Maryland dates back to 1648, to a Frenchman named Tenis Palee. Not much is known about Palee except that he was from New Albion Colony, an English colony that stretched from New Jersey down through Pennsylvania to Maryland. He was said to have made eight different types of wines from four different grapes, including Muscat.

Fourteen years later, in 1662, Lord Baltimore had a goal of planting vines and making wine. There are two stories about what happened to Lord Baltimore's vineyard. Some say that three hundred acres of vines were planted and all died. The other story says that the vines never survived the trek from Europe and so were never planted at the land grant called "The Vineyard." There is also reference to a grape grower named William Hutchinson in 1689, but not much of his story is known.

Over a century after Lord Baltimore and William Hutchinson made their attempts, Colonel Benjamin Tasker Jr. tried his hand at grape growing and winemaking, a bit more successfully. In 1756, Tasker planted his small vineyard, about two acres at his sister's estate in Prince George's County.

This vineyard, in a town now called Belair, included the Alexander grape. Alexander had only been found a mere fifteen years prior to this by James Alexander near Philadelphia. In a letter from Governor Horatio Sharpe to Lord Baltimore, Sharpe says:

> *There hath been no Burgundy made in Maryland since my arrival except two or three hogsheads which Col Tasker made in 1759 this was much admired by all that tasted it in the months of February and March following, but in a week or two afterwards it lost both its Colour & Flavour so that no person would touch it & the ensuing winter being a severe one destroyed almost all the Vines.*

The wine was tasted by Reverend Andrew Burnaby in Philadelphia, who claimed that the wine was "not bad." This devastating winter referenced in Lord Baltimore's letter was in the year 1760, and just one year later, Colonel Tasker passed away at the age of forty.

Governor Horatio Sharpe, Maryland's governor from 1753 to 1758, was interested in the cultivation of grapes and was fond of European varieties. Ten years after Tasker's death, in 1770, Charles Carroll planted vineyards at his family estate, Doughoregan Manor, near Ellicott City. Carroll planted four grape varieties here: "Rhenish, Virginia grape, Claret and Burgundy." Doughoregan Manor remains in the Carroll family. The family re-planted vineyards in 1971, and the fruit was sold to Philip Wagner at Boordy Vineyards.

According to *A History of Horticulture in America*, as cited by Thomas Pinney in *A History of Wine in America*, there are records of advertisements placed by nurserymen who were trying to sell vinifera grapes to Marylanders right up to the time of the Revolutionary War.

JOHN ADLUM: THE FATHER OF AMERICAN VITICULTURE

This documentation would be remiss if it did not mention the most notable records of grape growing and winemaking dating before the twentieth century. A man named John Adlum, known, as the "Father of American Viticulture," was first a solider and then a major in the American Provisional Army during the Revolutionary War. For the purposes of this story, Adlum was most notably an advocate for agriculture, specifically the grape, and was active in urging the foundation of federally funded viticulture research programs. He planted his first vineyard in Havre de Grace, Maryland—at what is now called Swan Harbor—before moving his research efforts to a plot of land in the District of Columbia.

In Washington, D.C., Adlum planted the Vineyard, a two-hundred-acre plot of both domestic and vinifera grapevines. He wrote two books on grape growing and winemaking: *A Memoir on the Cultivation of the Vine and the Best Mode of Winemaking* in 1823 and *Adlum on Making Wine.*

In *A Memoir on the Cultivation of the Vine*, Adlum says

> *I made a Wine of the Schuylkill Muscadell, (near Havre de Grace, where the Vines grow on a rich loam well manured, and with a clay bottom;) which was pronounced equal to the best Wine of France. And this was not complimentary, but a fact; for it was put upon the table with one of the best Wines that France produces; and no one could tell which was the French, or which was American; neither could they perceive a difference. It is but proper to remark, that I never made quite such good wine since, owing to some accidental and unaccountable circumstance, in the making of the first.*

The Schuylkill Muscadell grape that Adlum references is the same grape that Benjamin Tasker planted: the Alexander. In his book, Adlum references "an uncommonly large Fox-Grape, from a neighbourhood of Elkton, Maryland; it has a very musky smell, and is full of a beautiful red juice. I have not yet had enough of them to make Wine." While the variety is unknown, this was one of the twenty varieties he grew in the Washington, D.C. vineyard.

Adlum also was largely responsible for propagating a grape known as Catawba—a grape that would later become the most widely planted grape in the country in the nineteenth century. As the story goes, he found the vines at the home of a Mrs. Schell in Clarksburg, Montgomery County, Maryland, and took cuttings. The widow's late husband grew these grapes, but no one could remember where they came from in order to tell Adlum. It was thought that the grapes came from North Carolina. The widow called them Catawba, and Adlum determined that the grapes were not European and may have actually been hybrids.

Adlum later supplied cuttings of this variety to Nicholas Longworth in Ohio, who made the grape famous. Adlum said, "In bringing this grape to public notice, I have rendered my country a greater service then [*sic*] I would have done had I paid off the national debt."

Adlum often corresponded with friend Thomas Jefferson—a fellow oenophile—about both grape growing and winemaking. In fact, Jefferson requested clippings from Adlum's vineyard to plant at Monticello, Jefferson's estate in Virginia. In reference to Adlum's Catawba wine, Thomas Jefferson said:

> *I received the two bottles of wine you were so kind as to send me. The first, called Tokay, is truly a fine wine, of high flavor, and, as you assure me, there was not a drop of brandy in it; I may say it is a wine of good body of its own. The second bottle, a red wine, I tried when I had good judges at the table. We agreed it was a wine one might always drink with satisfaction, but of no particular excellence.*

The first wine Jefferson refers to, the Tokay, was Adlum's name for his Catawba wine.

In the same decade that Adlum made his discoveries, legislation was passed to create a corporation called the Maryland Society for Promoting the Culture of the Vine. Written in the 1828–29 session laws is the following statement:

> *William M'Donald, Henry W. Rogers, Zebulon Waters, John C.S. Monkur, Philip Poultney, James Cox, William Gibson, John B. Morris, Richard G. Belt, Benjamin I. Cohen, George Fitzhugh, junior, Charles C. Harper, William G. Jones, Walter Price, Robert Sinclair, James R. Williams and Richard Caton, that they are desirous of being incorporated, the purpopse of introducing into the state of Maryland, and into our country generally, the extensive cultivation of the vine.*

The law stated that the corporation should have three hundred shares of ten dollars each. It was to have twelve directors, a president, a vice-president, a treasurer, a recording secretary and a corresponding secretary. The president and vice-president were to purchase land suitable for the "cultivating, improving, preparing, gathering and preserving, the grape, as also for the manufacture and preservation of the wine." The act was written to continue until 1860.

The original corporation may have faced challenges because on March 2, 1842, thirteen years later, a second act was passed. This new act was written to revive the Society for the Culture of the Vine. The law indicated that the new act would enable the corporation to dispose of old real estate that had belonged to the group in its former existence and to settle the concerns of the company. It also indicated that the board should be changed from having twelve directors down to six directors and that the officer positions of vice-president and corresponding secretary would be abolished.

According to *Pioneering American Wine*, this Society for the Culture of the Vine was part of a larger conversation about grape growing and winemaking in the United States and had tasted the wines of Nicholas Herbemont, one of the earliest winemakers in the country. Editor David S. Shields says that one of the concerns of the Maryland society "was the medical use of wine for stomach ailments, and the delicacy of Herbemont's white wine struck the group as ideal for such applications." In a letter published by *American Farmer*, this group said that the wine had "the most delicate and delicious flavored of any we ever tasted. We tested its quality pretty extensively, having expended a considerable sample of it among epocures in the article, all of whom without an exemption, pronounced it *particularly fine*." The society was formed after the group tasted Herbemont's 1827 vintage. Shields goes on to say that the Maryland vineyard planters and wine drinkers were interested in Herbemont's winemaking process, from the vineyard to the bottle. In fact, Herbemont wrote an entire essay for the Baltimore-based Society of the Culture of the Vine. It was later published by Hitchcock in Baltimore in 1833.

One of the members of the Society for the Culture of the Vine, not listed in the session law, was named Dr. John W. Fendell "Pomonkey." Shields notes in his record of Herbemont's writings that Pomonkey derived his name from Pomonkey in Charles County, overlooking the Potomac River. He says, "Benjamin Fendell II had named his plantation in that county 'Pomonkey' in the eighteenth century. I presume the vintner who addressed Herbemont was a descendant who resided in Charles County, yet visited often in Baltimore, staying perhaps at Woodlawn, home of Dr. Edward Fendall." Shields goes on to tell the story of a letter written by this Pomonkey on February 18, 1832, which stated that he had twenty acres of vineyard. The vineyard was made of vinifera and even had cuttings from Chateau Haut Brion in France.

Herbemont was so close with the Society for the Culture of the Vine that he was elected an honorary member after its formation. In a letter to Edward Stabler, a postmaster in Sandy Spring, Maryland, Herbemont notes that he gave the following grapes to George Fitzhugh, his closest friend in Baltimore:

"Madeira"—"Bordeaux table grape," called by some here "Hungarian," "Bosx." This I named from a gentleman in France. "Sauvignon," "Olivette," "Melier," "Deo-data." This I named after one of my brothers Dieudonné, and "Lafitte"…I am much obliged to you for your kind offer of cuttings of such vines as I may want and you may have; but the obligingness of Mr. Fitzhugh has scarcely left me anything to desire in this respect.

After these events, the history of the Maryland wine industry becomes very quiet. It is not until the next century that the country goes through an alcohol overhaul and we meet the next grape growing and winemaking pioneer of Maryland, Philip Wagner.

Chapter 2
Prohibition and the New Deal Winery

PROHIBITION

Wine has enjoyed increasing popularity throughout the period of prohibition. I have even heard it suggested that if prohibition were to continue in force for another decade, we might reasonably expect the United States to become a wine-drinking nation. For this paradox we must thank our legislators, who with wisdom and humanity have permitted the making of naturally fermented fruit juices in the home, without unpleasant legal consequences, and so have helped to temper the rigours of an unsuccessful experiment.

These are the words of Maryland's first ever commercial winery owner, Philip Wagner, in his book, *American Wines and How to Make Them*, originally published in 1933, just as Prohibition was repealed.

Prohibition was a federally enforced regulation. Individual states were granted "concurrent law," meaning they could pass their own laws enforcing prohibition that were at least as strict as the federal law stated, if not more restrictive. Maryland was the only state that refused to pass *any* concurrent legislation or state enforcement act of supporting Prohibition.

Many Maryland residents and politicians alike were not in favor of Prohibition. United States congressman John Philip Hill, in fact, was indicted with charges of making wine and cider during Prohibition. As Thomas Pinney describes in his book *A History of Wine in America*, Hill was an outward opponent of Prohibition. Hill's goal was to challenge language in the bill that referred to home winemaking and brewing. Hill's issue with the law was that city residents didn't have the same rights as farmers, who could ferment their fruit into cider reaching an alcohol level of 2.75 percent, when other residents—city dwellers without land and space to grow fruit trees—couldn't purchase anything over half of 1 percent legally. An article in the *Baltimore Sun* on August 22, 1923, read:

> *Congressman John Philip Hill today served formal and solemn notice on the Probation Commissioner and the Collector of Internal Revenue for Maryland that on or about noon, September 7, he will begin producing non-intoxicating fruit juices for use in his home. His intention is to get from the prohibition department a definition of "non-intoxicating" as used in the Volstead Act.*
>
> *When the new regulations concerning the manufacture for home use of cider and similar fruit juices were issued; he said, "I expect to find the definition in them. But after reading them carefully I find that 'non-intoxicating' is defined simply as 'non-intoxicating.'*
>
> *So I'm going up in the country and get some grapes and go down on Baltimore Street and get a press, and I'm going to start making grape juice. I have written the Prohibition Commissioner to ask him just when I should stop fermentation. In his answer I expect to learn after two years of inquiry just when a beverage ceases to be non-intoxicating and becomes intoxicating."*

Hill was clearly trying to make a point. One of the notable facts about this effort was a picture following this article a few days later. The photos showed Hill with baskets of Anne Arundel County grapes. In this article, Hill said, "In making my grape juice I will follow the directions of the Department of Agriculture." This means two things—Hill was pushing the envelope, and grapes were being grown in the seat of the state capital, Anne Arundel County, around the time of Prohibition.

Hill went a step further and started Franklin Farms in a courtyard adjoining his Baltimore city home. He had tied apples onto trees, which would become his "orchard," from which he would make cider, fermented up to 2.75 percent, which was allowed by the Volstead Act.

He was eventually indicted for the manufacturing of alcohol but was not found guilty. It was Hill's efforts that helped to clarify that home winemaking was legal—an important moment in this story, as it would later allow Maryland's first winery owner the right to make wine at home.

Other Marylanders played roles in the anti-Prohibition movement. Governor Albert C. Ritchie, for example, was outwardly in favor of the "wets" and wanted residents to make their own moral decisions about alcohol. Baltimore's own H.L. Mencken, although not a politician but rather a public figure, was a friend of Governor Ritchie and was known to celebrate the repeal of Prohibition. These different examples tie directly into the beginning of the modern Maryland wine industry in the moving forward of Philip Wagner, one of H.L. Mencken's friends from the *Baltimore Sun*.

Wagner was working as an editorial writer at the *Baltimore Sun* while Mencken was an editor—an editor who was an advisor to Governor Ritchie. While one can only speculate, it was possible that Wagner was involved in the many discussions of Prohibition repeal between Mencken and Ritchie, which may have been an influence on Wagner's own home winemaking.

Because of the efforts of Governor Ritchie and Philip Hill, Maryland residents were able to make wine at home, and Wagner was able to move his research and study to propel the vine and the grape. From there, an industry blossomed.

Maryland lived up to its nickname, the "Free State," during Prohibition, too. Much later, Hamilton Owens, editor of the *Baltimore Sun*, used the nickname in a different context. In 1923, Georgia congressman William D. Upshaw, a firm supporter of Prohibition, denounced Maryland as a traitor to the Union for refusing to pass a state enforcement act. Mr. Owens thereupon wrote a mock-serious editorial entitled "The Maryland Free State," arguing that Maryland should secede from the Union rather than prohibit the sale of liquor. The irony in the editorial was subtle, and Mr. Owens decided not to print it. He popularized the nickname, however, in later editorials.

THE NEW DEAL WINERY

After the repeal of Prohibition, it was thought among some circles that a vibrant wine industry could be part of the United States' revitalization through an industry similar to that in European countries. President Franklin Delano Roosevelt and one of the members of his "brain trust," an agricultural economist and assistant secretary of agriculture at the time, Rexford Tugwell, conducted this train of thought.

The United States Department of Agriculture housed a research center in Beltsville, Maryland, beginning in 1913. This research center, located in Prince George's County, neighbors Washington, D.C. Previously the Walnut Grange plantation, this center was first used as an animal husbandry research site. Tugwell directed the building of a state-of-the-art winery on the grounds of the Beltsville Research Center. The winery was built into a hillside to make use of gravity flow. It included several production rooms, including refrigerated fermenting rooms, six underground storage cellars, a bottling room and even a brandy still. A similar winery was built at another research station in Mississippi. According to Leon Adams's *The Wines of America*, Tugwell even went so far as to send representatives to Europe to collect yeast cultures to prepare for this initiative. Tugwell also had interesting ideas about refraining from taxing beer and wine in order to dissuade the consumption of liquor.

Sadly, the winery was never used. When Congress learned of the project, it froze funding and, with it, all plans. Congressman Clarence Cannon, a Mississippi representative, was part of the brick wall that blocked the progress of the winery. In fact, he threatened to block all Department of Agriculture funding if the project were to move forward. The space is now used to grow various test crops in controlled temperatures and is called the West Building. According to Adams, the crusher-stemmer from Beltsville found its way to Hallcrest Vineyard in California.

Chapter 3

On the Shoulders of Giants

There is no one I would rank higher for his contributions to grape growing east of the Rockies than Philip Wagner." This is what the dean of American enologists, Maynard A. Amerine, was quoted as saying in an article from the *American Wine Society Journal* in 1989. "No one has done more in the last 50 years for wine and grapes than Philip Wagner," said Walter S. Taylor of Bully Hill Vineyards in the same article.

Philip Wagner was born in New Haven, Connecticut, on February 18, 1904. He graduated from the University of Michigan with his AB degree and then moved to Shenectady, New York, as a young man. It was there that he worked for the General Electric Company for five years. In 1930, Wagner moved to Maryland to work for the *Baltimore Sun* newspaper.

Wagner was an editorial writer from 1930 until 1936 at the *Baltimore Sun* and was then promoted to become the London correspondent for the paper for one year. With his new position, Wagner spent time in both London and Baltimore. He later became editor of the *Evening Sun* from 1938 to 1943 and finished his time there as editor from 1943 to 1964.

Wagner was a wine drinker from the start, as his parents drank wine with their meals. Wagner and some friends, including H.L. Mencken, became interested in making their own wine during Prohibition, when the American public was given two options: drink no wine or drink what you can make in your own home. At first, he used grapes that were shipped in from California—zinfandel and Carignane, namely, according to *The Wines of America* by Leon Adams. In an interview in the Maryland Grape Growers

Philip Wagner with wine thief in hand, testing the wine's progress. *Courtesy of Boordy Vineyards.*

Association (MGGA) newsletter, Philip Wagner said, "We paid the $50 for a license to become winemakers. We made some wine in 5-gallon lots, using whatever materials we could find."

Wagner began his own experimental vineyard on a piece of property that he rented in Riderwood, Maryland, that coincidentally housed the remains of a tiny vineyard—about twenty vines—when he and his wife, Jocelyn, moved there. A year later, he purchased that property and planted his own vines, all vinifera, which all failed. His lack of success with vinifera grapes led to his belief that vinifera could not be grown on the East Coast due to the cold winters, muggy summers and the vines' tendency to rot. According to an article in the *American Wine Society Journal* by Hudson Cattell and Linda Jones McKee, Wagner searched for more varieties of grapes in places like Geneva, New York; Denison, Texas; and even Missouri.

A Full-Bodied History

During his time in London, Wagner discovered hybrid wine grapes—grapes that are a cross of vinifera and Native American grapes. According to the previously mentioned *American Wine Society Journal* article, Wagner sought out information about the hybrids at the East Maling agricultural station in London. The people at this agricultural station were researching these hybrids for their ability to survive cold weather. In fact, they referred to them as "cold country vinifera." Wagner thought these might not only be stable in cold climates but also may be resistant to the disease that his vinifera faced in Riderwood. Wagner brought some of these hybrids, like Baco Noir and Vidal Blanc, and planted them in his own vineyard. He found that they "made wines that taste like wine," which was his goal, as Wagner was put off by the foxy taste of native labrusca varieties.

Wagner certainly legally imported vines through France's Department of Agriculture, but rumor has it he might have also snuck in some vines. As the story goes, Wagner and Jocelyn may have actually smuggled cuttings of Vidal Blanc from France back to the United States. The legend, as told by Robert Deford Jr., current owner of Boordy Vineyards, is as follows:

> *In the early '30s, Phil was a correspondent in Europe during pre–World War II anxiety and buildup. He was traveling in France with Jocelyn, and they came across Vidal in the backyard of Monsieur Vidal himself in Cognac and got cuttings. Phil was actively collecting vines because he felt that he needed to start a Johnny Appleseed rebellion against Prohibition by getting backyard vineyardists going…So they collected the Vidal Blanc vines from Monsieur Vidal. They put it in Jocelyn's purse, and according to Phil, they kept it moist in the bidets at night as they traveled around France and they brought the first Vidal vines to America, unbeknownst to any plant inspectors.*

Using his knowledge of wine and his background in writing, Wagner wrote various articles and books on winemaking. One of his first articles on American wine was published in the magazine the *American Mercury*. After his retirement from the *Baltimore Sun*, Wagner would continue to write articles about wine and public affairs.

It wasn't long after that Wagner's "Johnny Appleseed" movement continued in book form when he wrote the first modern book in English about winemaking, called *American Wines*, which was published in 1933, the same year Prohibition was repealed. All the other available books about grape growing and winemaking were written in French, so Wagner's book was widely distributed and used by many.

A letter from the French Department of Agriculture identifying the hybrid grapes imported to the United States of America for use by Philip Wagner. *Courtesy of Boordy Vineyards.*

Boordy Nursery

These books and writings became a Bible to winemakers across the nation. Warren Winiarski, owner and winemaker of Stags Leap Wine Cellars, celebrated for its Cabernet Sauvignon in the famed Judgment of Paris, studied under Wagner. "I'm proud to say that he was my first and constant teacher," Winiarski was quoted in Wagner's obituary. "I was very heavily influenced in my decision to take up the trade when I read Phil's book." Winiarski spent some time in Maryland, where he met both his wife and Wagner. "I made my first wines from grapes that I got from one of his farmers out in Westminster in the 1950s," Winiarski said.

Not only did Wagner propagate the *word* of the vine, but he also began to propagate the actual vines. Once Wagner's ideas and words extended to other grape growers and winemakers, they came asking questions about these new French hybrids (called American hybrids in France, oddly enough). Eventually, a demand for these hybrid grapes was developed, and Wagner filled the void. He began selling these vines, and his operation became known as Boordy Nursery. His vines were sold all over the East Coast, the mid-Atlantic and even the West Coast and Canada.

In 1940, Philip Wagner married his wife Jocelyn. Jocelyn and Philip were both musicians. "If you came in unannounced, you would hear the piano

A collection of grape clusters at the Maryland State Fair. This display includes twenty varieties of grapes, including unusual varieties like Mill, Diamond and Westfield. *Courtesy of Boordy Vineyards.*

and the violin playing," said family friend and future owner of Boordy Vineyards Rob Deford. Deford recalls fond memories of Jocelyn playing the piano and Philip on the violin. "You would be offered bread and cheese and a glass of Boordy wine. You would enjoy great conversation. They were erudite, fascinating people."

The Wagners' love affair with the grape and the wines they produced extended far beyond their home.

BOORDY VINEYARDS

As it happens in the home grape-growing and winemaking business, there are often too many grapes and not enough buyers or thirsty individuals in the household, and so wineries are born. In 1945, Philip and Jocelyn Wagner opened Boordy Vineyards at their Riderwood property. They grew various grape varieties on their small, five-acre vineyard. Wagner called the winery "America's first winery dedicated to producing wines from French-American hybrid grapes." This same year, he published his second book, *A Wine-Growers Guide*. Always the clever wordsmith, Wagner wrote the following promotional copy for the new Boordy Vineyards:

> *Just north of Baltimore, at the end of a lane near the village of Riderwood, is a white stuccoed building with barn-red trim. There are grape vines to the right of it, and more vines on the slope up beyond it. The aspect is not greatly different from that of a typical small French wine-growing property, say in the Beaujolais country, the scene is rural Maryland. This is the winery, vineyard and nursery of Boordy Vineyard, the property of J. &P. Wagner.*
>
> *Over the hill a mile away, on the southern slope of the famed Green Spring Valley, there is a larger vineyard. Drive up Route 140 to Westminster, and on the right just before entering town you may catch a glimpse of the Lussier vineyard. Go up into Harford County, and beyond Bel Air on a back road between Churchville and Aberdeen the Vinson vineyard is to be found. These vineyards and several others scattered about the State, and planted with vines which Boordy Vineyard has provided from its own nursery and which have been selected for their ability to yield good red and white table wines in Maryland. The vintages from these vineyards, blended together, yield the Boordy wines.*

The selection of these grape varieties, which are called French hybrids and which are new to the United States, is a story in itself, but one too long to tell here. Sufficient to say that the work of selection has been going on for a good many years. The vineyards, the winery—and the wine—are the outgrowth of the Wagners' work in fitting the right grapes to Maryland's soil and climate.

Boordy Vineyards is a very small winery. Mr. and Mrs. Wagner call it the "worlds smallest," and perhaps it is. It is also the only winery in Maryland producing table wines from Maryland-grown grapes. The pleasant Maryland country side contains much good vineyard land and could one day become a new wine-growing region, the source of light still and sparking lines with a character quite their own. But such developments come slowly. In the meantime, the Wagner's like to think that with the wines and vines of Boordy Vineyard they are starting to add a new crop to the agriculture of these parts and opening a new chapter in the story of Good Living in Maryland.

As to the wine—

We can recommend particularly the white wine of the current vintage. It is greenish-gold in color, and fresh-tasting. It is light in body, yet a trifle sweet (the vintages vary in Maryland, as they do in Europe). It will be relished by those who enjoy a French Graves or medium-sweet Sauternes, yet it is inexpensive. It goes well with seafood, chicken, "made dishes," sandwiches, fruits, nuts, cheese—and it should be served very cold. Why not try a bottle? Or, better yet, a case to keep on hand for Special Occasions, late snacks, emergency entertainment.

In an article called "Vin Ordinaire as an Elegant Avocation" in the Style section of the *Washington Post*, author Judith Martin described rules that the Wagner family had set for themselves in regard to the grape and wine business:

The first is that the vineyard, in which the original idea was to provide wine for the family table, and the nursery, with which they demonstrated that respectable wine could be produced in country which had been deemed unsuitable, should pay for themselves. The second is that it should not interfere with the rest of the Wagner's activities. Boordy, for all its success, is, after all, the rather elegant hobby of people whose lives are concerned first with politics and writing. Wagner says it's his version of another man's sailboat or herd of prize cattle.

A photo of Philip and Jocelyn Wagner in the vineyard. *Courtesy of Boordy Vineyards.*

It should be noted that this wasn't a one-man show. Jocelyn, Philip's wife, was more than behind the scenes. She was a partner in this business and even participated in making wine deliveries to retail outlets. Her name and initial was included everywhere, as was his: "J&P Wagner." Jocelyn was famous for posing in action photographs in the winery—working at the bottling line, in the vineyard and near the barrels.

Wagner made about eight thousand gallons of wine a year and distributed it to restaurants and wine shops in the Baltimore and Washington, D.C. area, and eventually the wine was sold as far north as New York. According to Boordy Vineyards' website, Wagner recalled that the first shipment of his wine to Macy's in New York drained his inventory: a whopping forty cases of wine.

In 1968, Boordy Vineyards partnered with Seneca Foods Corporation in New York and Washington states. In 1974, Seneca Foods approached Wagner about purchasing the Boordy name. The brand was to expand to be supplied by wineries in Yakim Valley, Washington and Penn Yan, New York. This arrangement only lasted for two years before the focus came back to the Riderwood vineyard and winery.

By the late 1970s, while the boutique winery concept was taking off, Boordy Vineyards was selling three types of wine—red, white and rosé. Wagner's wines were described as "impertinent, innocent, honest and floral" by Craig Claiborne in the *New York Times*.

The world-known viticulturist Lucie Morton has worked in vineyards all over the world, but her home is in Virginia. Yet Lucie is tied to Wagner's Boordy Nursery, as this is where her family purchased their first grapevines. About Wagner's wines, Lucie says, "Wagner's home vineyards had fairly minimal inputs by today's standards of canopy management

BOORDY VINEYARD
J. & P. Wagner, Props.
RIDERWOOD, MARYLAND

WHITE WINE (Dry)
BACO RED WINE

By the Bottle_____$1.50
Special price by the case

WINES

of the

REGION

The wise traveler will tell you that you don't go far wrong if you stick to the wines of the region. In Bordeaux, a bottle of claret or Sauternes; in Italy, a *fiasco* of chianti or a bottle of stout red Barolo; in San Francisco, one of the many good wines from the Coast Counties—and hereabouts, a bottle of Boordy Vineyard, red or white, grown and made in Maryland!

Have you tried the wines of these pioneer Maryland wine-growers? The *Dry White:* fresh as a Bay breeze, with a discreet but unforgettable aroma, good with almost anything but at its best with seafood. The *Baco Red:* an ingratiating companion to all manner of meats, poultry and "made" dishes. If you don't know these "wines of the region" you have a treat in store!

A piece of promotional material created by Philip Wagner for Boordy Vineyards. This is indicitave of his local focus, inspired by European wine consumption. *Courtesy of Boordy Vineyards.*

and produced simple table wines with endearing authenticity and lack of pretention. His wines were pure expression of a place—a cottage, not a McMansion."

Philip Wagner was a leader in the American wine industry and especially in the Maryland wine industry. He was the first to own a winery and impacted so many of the state wineries of today. Wagner's influence also reached other winemakers outside of Maryland, like Joseph Heitz of Heitz Cellars at St. Helena; Robert Mondavi; and his friend Dr. Maynard Amerein, known as the Father of American Wine. Wagner received the Mérite de Agricole award from the French Embassy for his work with hybrid grapes.

It should also be noted that Philip Wagner was involved in the politics of the state wine industry and was responsible for creating a fifty-dollar farm winery license fee for wineries that made product that used Maryland grapes.

THE VINIFERA-HYBRID DEBATE

It wasn't that Wagner didn't want to grow vinifera grape varieties; these varieties just did not succeed in his vineyard. His attempts were unsuccessful for a variety of reasons, including a lack of education, as well as less developed disease-fighting sprays and tools, now used regularly by East Coast grape growers. Hybrids were much more successful.

Wagner was famed for his writings and for bringing hybrids to the United States and the East Coast. He propagated them through his writings, spoken word and especially through his nursery. Wagner's beliefs about the successes and failures of hybrids and vinifera were challenged by other wine pioneers on the East Coast. His most prominent opposition was from Dr. Konstantin Frank, who proved that vinifera could thrive on the East Coast and thought that hybrids could be poisonous to humans. Because of Wagner's devotion to hybrids, this led to some major tension.

Wagner was quoted in an article in the *American Wine Society Journal*, from a discussion at an American Wine Society Conference, as saying, "I do not and never have seen any basis for controversy given the premise that we all want to produce the best wine we can out of the best grapes we can rely on, within the limits of our many different and frequently difficult climates. We can discover these limits only be taking advantage of the whole range of available grape materials."

Wagner created a place for wines made from hybrid grapes on the tables of the American people. He proved that hybrids do grow well on the East Coast and that yes, in fact, they can make wonderful wines. His legacy can be seen on the shelves of wine shops and in wineries all over the East Coast.

THE TRANSITION OF BOORDY VINEYARDS

In order to help his winery grow, Wagner branched out to network with other farmers around the state. He encouraged them to plant vines under his management. He supplied the vines and the advice and then purchased the grapes from his growers for use at the winery. The R.B. Deford family of Hydes, Maryland, became one of these growers in 1965 and after thirty-five years in the winery business, Jocelyn and Philip Wagner sold Boordy Vineyards to the R.B. Deford family in 1980. All the equipment was moved from their Riderwood property to the Deford family farm in Hydes. Wagner continued his nursery business after the winery was sold.

In 1995, when Boordy Vineyards celebrated its fiftieth birthday, the Deford family organized a book signing for Wagner. Anticipating a small turnout, Wagner was shocked at the line out the door. He sat at a stately mahogany desk and signed updated versions of the book he authored. Only two years later, Philip Wagner passed away. Emphysema and heart failure claimed his life at age ninety-two.

Philip Wagner once said, "Boordy...is one of those fine old Maryland place names of the future," and he was right.

HAM MOWBRAY AND MONTBRAY WINE CELLARS

"If it hadn't been for Phil's clear and lucid writing about winemaking and viticulture, I would never have become involved in the demanding, frustrating, physically exhausting yet so rewarding pursuit of the quintessential essence of the grape that we know as wine," Ham Mowbray once said. If there were two giants of the early Maryland wine industry, Philip Wagner was one and Hamilton Mowbray was the other. Modern-day wineries revel in stories of Ham and credit him with an enthusiastic approach and a desire to get others involved in the wine industry.

Hamilton Mowbray was born in Taylorsville, Maryland, on Christmas Eve 1921. The son of a minister, Mowbray moved around quite a bit. He enlisted in the U.S. Air Force at age twenty-one and was stationed in Guatemala. In 1946, at the age of twenty-three, Mowbray married Phyllis Louise Wagner and enrolled in Johns Hopkins University. He received his Bachelor of Science and Master of Science degrees by 1950.

Mowbray was then accepted to Cambridge University, where he and Phyllis lived for several years. Like Wagner, it was during Mowbray's years in England that his interest in wine was piqued. The availability of inexpensive wine and a few trips to France, first to Paris and then to Côte d'Azur, among other regions in the south of France, cemented his interest in and appreciation for French wine.

When Mowbray completed his studies in England, he and Phyllis moved back to Baltimore and began a family. He was working full time as a research psychologist at the Johns Hopkins Applied Physics Lab in Scaggsville, Maryland. The Mowbrays moved to a house in Woodbine with about three acres of land. At that point, Mowbray met Emile Lussier and later Charles Singleton, both grape growers for Philip Wagner.

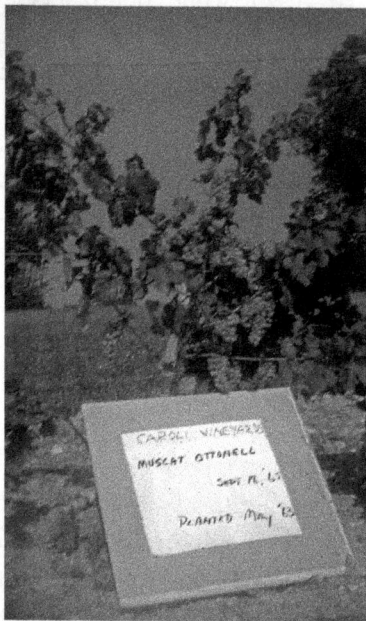

A young muscat vine at Charles Singleton's Caroli Vineyard. *Courtesy of Leslie A. Hubbard.*

Mowbray toured Lussier's vineyard and learned about grapes, and Singleton gave Mowbray some vine cuttings to start his own vineyard in Woodbine. According to an interview in the Maryland Grape Growers Association newsletter, the first vines Mowbray planted were Ravat 262, Seibel 13053, Seyve-Villard 5276 (also known as Seyval) and Foch. He then started making wine in his basement.

Concurrently, Charles Singleton was getting ready to open Maryland's second winery. Singleton spent a lot of time in Italy and developed a taste for food and wine. He bought a farm, which he named "The Farm." Here he planted vegetables for his own consumption, as well as grapes. After meeting Mowbray, Singleton opened the second winery in Maryland, called Caroli Winery. Mowbray worked at the Caroli Winery with Singleton until Singleton decided to close the winery and sell his equipment to Mowbray for his use at what would become Montbray Wine Cellars. Singleton then began to sell Mowbray his grapes.

The Mowbrays' first child, Paul, was born in 1954, followed by sister Claire in 1958.

In 1964, the Mowbray family bought a run-down dairy farm in Silver Run and called it the Resurvey on High Germany. Drawn in by the south-facing slopes and the well-drained, schist-filled soil, Ham wasn't deterred by the work that needed to be done to the old farm and

A shot of Ham Mowbray and Charles Singleton harvesting Foch grapes into recycled crab bushels before grape lugs were commonly used during harvest in Maryland. ©*Estate of Hamilton Mowbray. Used by permission.*

farmhouse. He had several friends who helped him turn the barn into a winery and a steady stream of volunteers who eventually pitched in to help with each harvest's picking, pressing, crushing and bottling. All were well fed by his wife, Phyllis, whom Mowbray called "indispensable." Phyllis did more than just feed the many winery guests. She managed the finances and made significant contributions to sales, advertising and promotion efforts. She and the children also helped with the vineyard tasks, bottling and labeling. Phyllis would always have a pot of soup on or would be entertaining on the screened-in porch. She was known for her revolving kitchen door. She was constantly feeding the many visitors, digging up flowers from her garden for them to take home and doing the bookkeeping for the winery business.

The name Montbray came from Mowbray's lineage. His ancestors, of Norman heritage, were called the De Montbrays, and so the name came. Montbray Wine Cellars opened in 1966.

It was here, at the farm in Silver Run, that the Mowbrays hosted many meetings and competitions for the newly formed American Wine Society. Mowbray could be found showing visitors—they were many and came often—around the winery, speaking to his dog in French or hiding away in his "office," a small building located between the house and the winery building.

THE FRANK EFFECT

One of Mowbray's initial connections to the world of wine was the famed Dr. Konstantin Frank. Dr. Frank was the pioneer of vinifera grapes of the eastern United States. In 1966, Mowbray joined other industry members at Dr. Frank's home on Keuka Lake in New York. This meeting was the unofficial founding of the American Wine Society (AWS). The AWS was officially founded the following year. Soon after, Mowbray founded one of the Maryland chapters.

From Frank, Mowbray got cuttings of Cabernet Sauvignon, Cabernet Franc, Chardonnay, Riesling and Pinot Noir, which he grafted onto rootstock from California. While some of the wine and grape community thought that Ham Mowbray was anti-hybrid, like Frank, this is incorrect. Mowbray proved that vinifera could, and did, grow well in Maryland with the proper care, but he also understood the value of hybrids. "I'll defend the place of hybrids in any vineyard. They're reliable, and make a good learning experience for those just starting out," said Mowbray in an interview in the *Maryland Grapevine*. "They're easy to grow and make decent wines. Then, when you get the feel of it, you can go onto other things." Viticulturist Lucie Morton has said, "Ham was a welcome bridge over the ubiquitous divide between viticulture based on European-American hybrids and European vinifera varieties."

MONTBRAY WINE CELLARS

Montbray Wine Cellars opened its doors in 1966. When it came to winemaking, Mowbray was an anti-interventionist. He created artisanal wines—wines that spoke for themselves. Bert Basignani, owner and winemaker of Basignani Winery, recalls asking Mowbray for advice. Unsure what to do with a finicky wine, Mowbray told Basignani to "give the wine a chance, it will balance itself out."

Like Philip Wagner, Mowbray looked to France for guidance. For example, he liked the idea of large oak barrels for first fermentation. Mowbray was known for his Seyval development but would only refer to the grape as SV-5276. He planted it extensively, as it was abundant and resistant to mold. It took well to his vineyard site, and eventually, he grafted it onto American rootstock.

Ham Mowbray in his cellar testing the recent vintage. ©*Estate of Hamilton Mowbray.* Used by permission.

Mowbray also taught classes on tasting wine and was described by John Wilcox in an article in the *Washington Post* on May 13, 1976, as a "ubiquitous figure on the local tasting scene, teaching public and private courses and lecturing frequently." On this specific newspaper clipping in Ham's personal collection, the word "ubiquitous" was circled in red pencil with an arrow that was written "Really?" in script. Ham must not have realized his reach.

Mowbray taught evening courses composed of four weekly three-hour classes to about sixty students each. These classes were conducted at the University of Maryland, University College, as well as the Mount Vernon College, near Washington, D.C., and at night classes associated with the Roland Park Country school near Baltimore. Ham also taught classes from an office in Columbia, Maryland, which he called the Montbray School of Wine. He taught more than just wine consumers. He shared with and taught winemakers—both in and out of state—through his writings, articles and presentations. Michael Dresser, wine critic of the *Baltimore Sun,* called him "the dean of the state's active winemakers" in an article in September 1990. Many of those winemakers would agree with that title.

SV-5276

While Mowbray loved vinifera, he also had an affinity for Seyval, or SV-5276. According to an article in the *Carroll County Bureau of the Sun* by Sheridan Lyons on Sunday, April 7, 1985, Mowbray and a plant physiologist named William Krul created "test-tube" grapes. Krul, then stationed at the U.S. Department of Agriculture's station at Beltsville, was a student in one of Mowbray's grape-growing classes at the University of

Maryland in 1975–76. According to the article, Mowbray and Krul took tissue from a vine cutting and placed the cells in a slurry. This slurry was put into a test tube, where the material created a callous, or cancerous, growth. Embroids from this growth were placed into another growing material and began to grow. The embroids began to grow roots and were planted into soil. Once they reached five to seven inches, they were placed in the vineyard. The article reported that the cloned vines thrived in the vineyard and produced taller vines, bigger bunches and grapes with balanced acid and sugar.

Because of Mowbray's work with the Seyval grape, the French embassy presented him with the Mérite Agricole award in 1975.

THE FIRST ICE WINE MADE IN THE UNITED STATES

On October 4, 1974, Ham Mowbray made the first ever American ice wine. It was early October, and Riesling grapes had been left on the vine at the Montbray Cellars vineyard. The temperature fell to twenty-two degrees and froze the grapes. Mowbray and his army of loyal friends handpicked the grapes, pressed them while frozen to extract the most concentrated juice and made one hundred bottles of the very first American ice wine, made in the traditional German style.

The press release that Mowbray sent from the winery announcing this unusual endeavor said:

> At dawn on the morning of October 4, 1974, the air temperature in Silver Run Valley, Maryland was 22 F. The Riesling grapes on a small section of Montbray Vineyards that had been left to develop the noble Botrytis mold were small frozen spheres. They were picked and pressed while still frozen to produce an authentic "Eiswein." So far as is known, no other commercial winery in the East has ever produced a Riesling of this sort. They may never do so again, since that is the lowest temperature ever recorded here on that date.

Ham and Phyllis continued their business as active industry members until 1992. They were an important part of the later formed Association of Maryland Wineries, and Ham had a permanent spot in the newsletter of the Maryland Grape Growers Association. Montbray Wine Cellars

A variety of labels from Montbray Wine Cellars. ©*Estate of Hamilton Mowbray. Used by permission.*

and Ham, especially, found the importance of the wine industry as a community. After Montbray Wine Cellars closed, Fred Wilson of Elk Run Vineyards managed Mowbray's vineyard for a number of years. Today, Bert Basignani manages the vineyard, which comprises over ten acres, made up of Seyval, Cabernet Sauvignon, Cabernet Franc and a recent planting of Nebbiolo.

THE AMERICAN WINE SOCIETY

The American Wine Society is the oldest consumer-based wine education organization in the United States and North America. The group was formed by a large group of wine enthusiasts in 1967 at Dr. Konstantin Frank's vineyard on Keuka Lake in New York. The first meeting was on October 7, 1967. Many Marylanders were involved in this organization from the beginning, including Ham and Phyllis Mowbray and their friends Les and Jean Hubbard. Over the years, the American Wine Society (AWS) has honored involved Marylanders. In 1976, Philip and Jocelyn Wagner received the AWS Award of Merit. In 1977, Ham Mowbray received the award. Maryland grape grower and USDA plant researcher Dr. John McGrew is a lifetime honorary member of the society.

The American Wine Society hosts conferences in different states each year. In 1971, the AWS came to Maryland, and the conference was held at the University of Maryland. Grape growers and home winemakers Les Hubbard and Al Copp served as co-chairs. Hubbard later worked

Hamilton Mowbray and Dr. Konstantin Frank discussing the virtues of whole cluster pressing Chardonnay in Frank's winery, where the press ran all day. *Courtesy of Leslie A. Hubbard.*

very closely with Mowbray at Montbray Wine Cellars, and Copp opened Woodhall Wine Cellars twelve years later. Al and Less scheduled cooking demonstrations for those conference attendees who didn't want to participate in the wine portion of the conference. The gathering then moved on to Detroit and various other locations.

At one of these historic gatherings, Dr. Konstantin Frank gave a revealing speech about how hybrids were dangerous to human beings and "proved" it through results from an experiment. Frank spoke of an experiment in which chickens were fed hybrid grapes, which resulted in the chickens giving birth to deformed chicks. Not long after, Maryland's own Ham Mowbray nullified this experiment and created a big debate between the two camps.

Chapter 4

The First Growth

In 1974, there were two wineries in Maryland, as Charles Singleton's Caroli Winery had closed. The third winery in Maryland was called Provenza Vineyard and was opened by Dr. Thomas Provenza and his wife, Barbara, in Montgomery County in 1974. They grew hybrid grapes, which were first planted in 1970. They were members of the American Wine Society, Maryland Chapter, and before opening their winery were longtime home winemakers. According to Leon Adams's book *Wines of America*, at one point the Provenza Vineyard had about fifteen acres that were taken care of by Lee and John Paul, who were horticulture students.

Linganore Winecellars at Berrywine Plantations

Provenza Vineyard was soon joined by a giant of the local wine industry. To say that Linganore Winecellars at Berrywine Plantation has been a heavy influence on the Maryland wine industry would be an understatement. Known for their its on-site wine festivals and sprawling wine portfolio of over twenty-five wines, the winery brings more than a party. Linganore Winecellars is a pillar in the history of Maryland wine. Responsible for bringing more hybrids to Maryland than any other active winery, Linganore has a vast history with humble beginnings and claims so many of Maryland's "firsts" in winemaking.

Owner Jack Aellen was born in Queens, New York, and has Swiss winemaking in his blood. He was taught how to make wine by his father in the basement of their home. Jack's wife, Lucille, the matriarch of this winery family, was raised in Brooklyn and has Italian winemaking in her family lineage. As an adult, Jack was a manufacturing chemist. He took a job in Maryland and moved with Lucille to a 230-acre farm in Mount Airy, just a few miles northeast of New Market. When Jack and Lucille left crowded New York City, their new home felt like a plantation to them because of its size and openness. They also did some research on grapes and learned that they were once called "wine berries." After switching the words around, the name Berrywine Plantation was born.

It was here that the Aellen family planted their first six acres of grapes in 1972. Originally, Jack and Lucille had planned a vineyard to supply enough grapes for their own home winemaking. Over time, they decided to become a commercial venture and opened their winery, Berrywine Plantations and Linganore Winecellars, in 1976.

Berrywine Plantations was formerly a dairy farm. The winery is located in a nineteenth-century post-and-beam barn on the property. The first year that Linganore Winecellars at Berrywine Plantation opened, they hand-processed six tons of grapes, using Lucille's father's equipment.

In the early years, Jack remembers winery visitors being very scarce. The family looked for ways to bring people out to the winery to try their wines and so developed a strong promotional program, including their annual wine festivals. In 1977, the winery hosted its first on-site wine festival. This was the first wine festival in the state.

In 1978, the Aellen family introduced semi-sweet grape wines and fruit and honey wines. The Aellen family worked very closely with Cornell University in New York. In the 1980s, Cornell had a hybrid-grape program in which it would look for farmers to plant test plots of different varieties. Test plots

The Silo at Berrywine Plantations. *Courtesy of Lucia Simmons, Linganore Winecellars at Berrywine Plantation.*

were secured in Missouri and Illinois, but Berrywine Plantation was the only test plot in Maryland. Linganore was very active in the program and planted a number of test varieties, many of which the winery—and now many other Maryland vineyards and wineries—still uses, including Traminette, Melody and the most popular, Cayuga. In the early 1980s, Jack and Lucille's sons, Anthony and Eric, took over the winemaking and vineyard management.

In 1983, the Aellen family applied for Maryland's first American Viticultural Area (AVA). This ninety square miles of land is called the Linganore Viticultural area and is federally designated. Two more AVAs were eventually designated, following the lead of the Linganore AVA.

The Aellen family was not and is still not afraid to experiment with their winemaking. They are known for their fruit wines, mead and even a dandelion wine. "People asked us if we could make it, and I looked at my son Anthony and said why don't we try?" Jack says. Meeting consumer demand is a priority at Linganore. They make wines that their customers enjoy. Linganore has also introduced dry fruit wines, a unique style in Maryland.

The original barn where wine manufacturing took place was replaced by a five-thousand-square-foot manufacturing space in 1997. Just two years later, a six-thousand-square-foot bottling area and tank room was created.

Linganore Winecellars' chocolate and wine pairing. *Courtesy of Lucia Simmons, Linganore Winecellars at Berrywine Plantation.*

In 2000, the winery purchased the state's first and only mechanical grape harvester. According to a written history created by the Aellen family, "We could now harvest in one hour what an eight man crew could harvest in one day, reducing time from harvest to processing to about 30 minutes."

Despite the fact that Jack Aellen was almost entirely blinded in a chemical explosion in 1957, he has been an immensely successful businessman, farmer and winemaker. His blindness has never set him back; rather, he has excelled in this industry. All of Jack and Lucille's children have been involved in the winery at some point. Son Anthony is the winemaker and president. Their younger son, Eric, is the vineyard manager. Lucia Simmons is the director of marketing. Anthony's daughter Melissa is studying winemaking at Cornell and will likely work in the family business at some point.

In 2011, the Aellens faced both triumph and disaster. The same year that they switched to using 100 percent wind power, a tornado did about $1 million of damage to their property. Anthony has joked, "We didn't order that much wind!" The roof of the production room was taken off the building. After enjoying the open sunlight, the Aellens decided to include windows in the newly constructed roof to let in the natural light, removing the need for electric light much of the year. This same year, Linganore installed a solar panel and electric car power stations—a first for a Maryland winery. They continue to take steps toward sustainability and remain stewards of the land.

The Aellens take pride in hard work and have gotten to where they are because of perseverance and wise business decisions. Anthony Aellen will often be heard saying, "We work smarter, not harder!" The Aellens are known for innovative winemaking techniques and old-fashioned inventiveness.

BON SPURONZA, BYRD, ZIEM AND THE CHESAPEAKE CIDER COMPANY

The next four wineries to open in Maryland have since closed, but they each played a role in the development of this brand-new industry. Bon Spuronza Winery opened in 1976 and was located near Westminster. The winery was owned by Ira Ross. He made the first "bag-in-a-box" wines in Maryland. The winery closed in 1982.

Byrd Winery was opened by pharmacist Bret Byrd and his wife, Sharon, a schoolteacher, in Mount Airy in 1976. They had a vineyard of about fifteen acres, all vinifera. The winery closed in 1996. Byrd Winery employed a

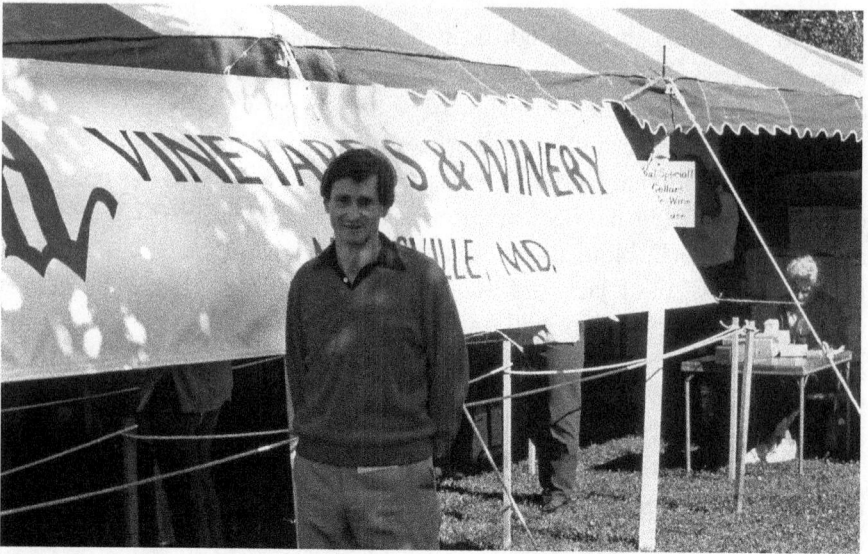

Bret Byrd, owner of Byrd Winery, in front of his sales and sampling tent at one of the first Maryland Wine Festivals. *Courtesy of Leslie A. Hubbard.*

winemaker named Bob Lyon, who would later go on to become owner of Catoctin Vineyards. Byrd was known for releasing some of the best Cabernet Sauvignons in the history of the state industry. Byrd's Cabernet Sauvignon received acclaim from Robert Parker and *Esquire* magazine in the 1980s. The wine was remarkable.

Bob and Ruth Ziem opened Ziem Wine Cellars in 1977 in Downsville, in Washington County. Before opening a winery, Bob was the director of solid propulsion for NASA Apollo Moon missions and later worked at the Pentagon. Upon planting vines and opening their winery, the Ziems focused exclusively on hybrid grapes, especially reds, and championed more unknown varieties like Landot Noir. The winery closed in 1998. Like Bret and Sharon Byrd, the Ziems were considered founding members of the Maryland wine industry.

Jim Case was the first cider producer in the state to obtain a winery license for his business, the Chesapeake Cider Company, which opened in 1984. Case purchased apples from local growers, and while his winery model didn't fit the traditional grapes-into-wine model, he was still fermenting a fruit juice. Chesapeake Cider Company was in business until it closed in 1990. This new cider-style winery model wasn't re-created until 2011.

THE DEFORD FAMILY'S BOORDY VINEYARDS

The R.B. Deford family owned a beef farm called Long Green Farm for generations. The farm is located in the Long Green Valley in Hydes, Maryland. They have occupied the property since the 1930s and raised everything from horses to grain, hay and even turkeys. Robert and Ann Deford were looking for alternative crops to cultivate, and under the guidance of their friend Philip Wagner, they started a nursery and small vineyard in 1965. Wagner supplied the nursery stock and advice for free and then purchased the fruit from the vineyard. The Defords were the very first commercial grape growers in Maryland and sold their grapes to Wagner—in the usual custom of a handshake deal.

The Deford vineyard was a "Wagner mix," with fifteen grape varieties in just five acres. Included were hybrid varieties but also vinifera varieties like Merlot and Aligoté. As a young man, Rob Deford Jr., son of Robert and Ann, was tasked with taking care of the vines during the summer. Looking back on the challenges of that time, Rob remembers using equipment fashioned out of old plumbing parts. Despite growing grapes for the godfather of hybrids, there was little research to learn from, and only the most forgiving grape varieties were successful. Within five years, the vineyard had failed due to very cold winters, a case of experiment neglect.

Rob Deford lived away from home for about fifteen years but came home from time to time to work at his family farm. The vineyard grew from 1965 to 1979, and Rob became more interested in the vineyard and winemaking process. He occasionally visited Wagner's Boordy in Riderwood and would watch how wine was made.

In the mid-1970s, Rob came back to the farm for good. His father, Robert, fell ill, and old farming methods were failing due to the new interstate system and four-season farming on the West Coast. The Deford family faced a crossroads and had to decide what to do with their family farm. Despite the fact that it was never in the family's long-range plans to get into the wine business, Rob saw a potential in wine that he thought could save the farm. He made a proposal first to his family and then to Philip Wagner to purchase Boordy Vineyards. Wagner accepted the offer the same weekend that Rob was accepted to the University of California–Davis's Viticulture and Oenology Department.

Rob left Maryland to start his education at UC–Davis and fell in love with California. As he was one of only three easterners, his West Coast counterparts were not afraid to share their trade secrets with a non-

Left: Rob Deford Jr. in the cellar. *Courtesy of Boordy Vineyards*.

Below: Philip Wagner watching over the move of equipment from Boordy Vineyards in Riderwood to Boordy Vineyards in Hydes. *Courtesy of Boordy Vineyards*.

threatening Marylander. Rob returned home to Long Green Farm in August 1980, the year that the Boordy purchase became complete. The newly reestablished winery received its federal permits, got electricity and brought the winery equipment from Riderwood to Hydes. The year 1980 brought about the first vintage from the new Boordy location.

Philip Wagner remained very supportive of the winery. He was able to watch the winery grow and change for sixteen years until he passed away.

The transition from Wagner's Boordy to today's Boordy Vineyards was not entirely smooth. In the late '80s, boutique wineries were taking off. Wagner's Boordy was generic. The winery offered a red, a white and a pink wine that sold at a very low cost from Maryland to Boston. It wasn't long after the Deford family bought Boordy that trucks of bad wine came back from New York and Boston. Rob knew something had to change.

Research about effective grape growing and winemaking became more readily available. Rob brought back a knowledge base from California and slowly learned what grapes he could grow. This "coming of age" for Rob resulted in an expansion from mainly hybrids to both hybrids and vinifera. The Deford family continued sourcing grapes from about six of Wagner's original growers. When speaking about the hybrid versus vinifera debate, Rob said, "I have one foot on Wagner's shoulders and one on Mowbray's. I owe something to each camp."

In 1983, Julie Colhoun came to work at Boordy as a hostess. It was here that she met Rob, and they began a relationship and married. Julie attended the first Maryland Wine Festival and, following in the tradition of equal partnership of Jocelyn and Philip Wagner, has been there for every step of Boordy's journey.

In 1984, Rob Deford became the first president of the Association of Maryland Wineries (AMW). Since that time, Rob has been a leader in the industry. He was chairman of Wine-America, the National Association of American Wineries, from 2000 to 2002 and then became president from 2002 to 2004. This leadership has made both Rob and Boordy Vineyards strong, standing pillars in the East Coast wine community.

Rob attributes much of Boordy Vineyards' modern growth to taking risks. After receiving his MBA from Loyola University Maryland's Sellinger School of Business in 1995, Rob learned that managing risks is key. He says, "You need to embrace risk for your company to grow. You have to be comfortable with that." He says that wineries as businesses can be successful, and he finds it exciting that the next generation can see this industry as a viable career opportunity.

In 1996, Boordy Vineyards signed a fifty-year lease on a property called South Mountain in Frederick County. This was a very large expansion of its vineyard property and is allowing the vineyard to continue efforts on a wine program called the "Landmark Project." The goal of this effort is to release a line of no-holds-barred, premium wines that are made from 100 percent Maryland fruit, sourced from newly planted and replanted vineyards.

In 2000, the Deford family donated their 240-acre easement to the Maryland Environmental Trust, a move that will preserve the farm and prohibit any development in the future. Rob calls that momentous occasion a real sign that the winery allowed his family to keep Long Green Farm.

Today, many Deford family members are still involved in the winery. Sally Buck, Rob's sister, and her husband, Bayly Buck, still live on the farm with Rob's mother, Ann. Phineas Deford, Rob's son, is now heavily involved in the family business.

Boordy has eighteen full-time employees and over one hundred part-time employees. The winery is recognized for its success on a national level. It is one of the largest wine producers in the state and a true icon of Maryland wine.

WOODHALL WINE CELLARS

Albert Copp was born and raised in Syracuse, New York, and graduated from Syracuse University with his MBA. He then moved to Washington, D.C., to work for the federal government and eventually moved to Baltimore, Maryland.

A wine drinker, Al had no interest in winemaking until the 1960s, when he attended a dinner put on by Harry's Wine Shop in Baltimore. It was there that he met two amateur winemakers who were both members of the Chesapeake Bacchus Club, a home winemaking group. One of the gentlemen at that dinner was Don Simmons, the man who later taught Al how to make wine and invited him to join the Chesapeake Bacchus Club.

Al first started making wines from kits. These wines were "drinkable, but awful," in his words. Unsatisfied with the quality of the concentrated wine, Al began to search for fresh grapes. He was able to track down Concord grapes for his use and for the Chesapeake Bacchus Club. The Bacchus Club was always looking for new grape sources. There are even rumors that the Bacchus Club pirated unripened grapes from one of Philip Wagner's vineyard sources to make their wine on occasion.

Al started looking for other vineyards from which to source. He would find grapes and bring them back to the Bacchus Club, and they would be divided up for use. Some of the Bacchus Club members would take the grapes home, and others would make their wine at Al's Roland Park home. He had a special air-conditioned and insulated garage behind the house just for winemaking.

Two members of the Bacchus Club, Mike DeSimone and Kent Muhly, became very close with Al. The three men decided to plant vines so that they could sell grapes to the Chesapeake Bacchus Club members. Their business plan was to grow twice as many grapes as they could use for their personal winemaking and sell the rest to cover their vineyard costs. Al and Mike DeSimone visited some land with a southern hillside on Belfast Road in Baltimore County owned by Realtor Herbert Davis, one of Al's friends. Al, Mike, Kent and Herbert agreed to form Woodhall Vineyards and planted three acres of grapes.

Today, Al looks back fondly on the Saturdays and Sundays spent at the vineyard. He and his partners would get most of their work done in the mornings and would enjoy lazy afternoons made up of big lunches—usually leftovers from the week prior—and plenty of wine.

Al's passion grew, and at one point, he even discussed partnership with fellow grape and wine enthusiast Ham Mowbray. While that partnership never came to fruition, Al did move forward with his dream of opening a winery with his partners, Mike, Kent and Herbert. A few years later, Woodhall Vineyards became Woodhall Vineyards and Wine Cellars, Inc., the ninth bonded winery in the state and opened in 1983, the same year that Elk Run Vineyards and Catoctin Vineyards opened.

The four partners worked hard on the winery business from 1983 until 1987, when tragedy struck. Mike DeSimone faced an untimely death in an automobile accident. That same year, Al's beloved wife also passed away. This was a hard time for Woodhall, and Al thought of closing the winery in 1989. It was then that the winds changed.

Chris and Pat Lang came to visit Woodhall and mentioned to Al that they were looking into buying a vineyard. The Langs worked with Al for a year, learning the business, and in 1999, they decided to buy the winery. Al was ready to leave the winery business and move in a new direction with his new wife, Laurie. Al sold the winery to Lang by way of a handshake and then went home and told his wife that he had sold the business. Challenging him,

Woodhall Wine Cellars owner Albert Copp. *Courtesy of Albert Copp.*

she told Al she didn't think he wanted to get out of the wine industry. She encouraged Al to go back to Chris Lang, and he did—buying back half the winery on a second handshake.

Now partners, Chris and Al looked toward the future of the winery. Chris Lang was living in New Jersey at this point and started looking for a home in Maryland. He found a home on York Road in Baltimore County—what would become the location of the modern-day Woodhall Wine Cellars.

Al and Chris hired another Chris, Chris Kent, to become winemaker at Woodhall. Woodhall sources grapes from local vineyards and produces both vinifera and hybrid wines and is still an active and successful winery. One of Woodhall's most recent victories was the release of a wine made from the Pinotage grape—a first for Maryland. The Pinotage was grown on the Eastern Shore by Jennie Schmidt and was made into a beautiful wine by Chris Kent. Most of the wine was sold in futures, but the winery looks forward to continuing this new addition to its product line. Woodhall is an active part of the Piedmont wine trail.

CATOCTIN VINEYARDS

Bob Lyon came to Maryland to be a pioneer of the East Coast wine industry. Originally from the Midwest, Lyon ventured east to Maryland in 1979 after studying winemaking at UC–Davis. He had worked with the famed winemakers from Chateau Montelena for fourteen months, as well as Domaine Chandon, Sebastiani Vineyards and Inglenook. Lyon played a major role in more Maryland wineries than any other winemaker of his time.

When he first arrived in Maryland, he took a job as winemaker at Byrd Vineyards. Lyon's time at Byrd concluded in 1982, at which point he began to work at various other vineyards. He started Catoctin Vineyards with his then girlfriend (now wife), Shahin Bagheri, and couples Jerry and Anne Milne and Roger and Judy Wolfe. Roger and Judy were already grape growers and active members of the Maryland Grape Growers Association. They planted a vineyard that included Chambourcin, Chancellor, Cabernet Sauvignon, Cabernet Franc and Riesling. They initially sold their grapes to Montbray Cellars before partnering with Lyon, Bagheri and the Milnes. To begin, Catoctin Vineyards was renting equipment from the now closed Provenza Vineyard.

Bob and Shahin bought the winery property and found that the years 1983, 1984 and 1985 proved to be great ones in the vineyard, and some great wines were made, according to Lyon. Catoctin Vineyards' preferred style of releasing wines was to hold them for years at a time to let them age. Bob recalls always having a large inventory of wines that could be sold over time.

"It takes tender loving care, proper aging, that sort of thing. Wine is pretty much made the same worldwide, but some are a little more reckless than others," said Bob Lyon in an article in the *Washington Post*. "I try to be on the other end." In this same article, reporter Elizabeth Williamson called the wines "artful,

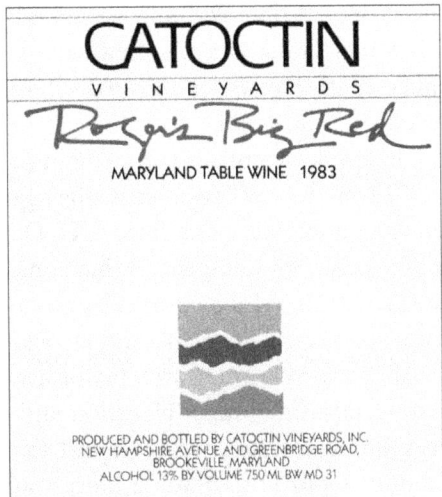

Roger's Big Red wine label, a representation of Catoctin Vineyards' modern label design. *Courtesy of Roger and Judy Wolfe.*

region-specific vintages, cultivated at Catoctin Winery." Yet even in 2005, Catoctin Vineyards' wine cost only eight to fifteen dollars a bottle. The winery produced about twenty-five thousand bottles a year.

Roger and Judy Wolfe sold their share of the winery in 1985, but the Milnes remained part of the business until they sold their share of the winery to Bob in 1999, from which point he and Shahin were sole proprietors. In 2006, Lyon sold the winery to a couple named Charlie Daneri and Emily Williams. Charlie and Emily lived on some property with a vineyard from which Catoctin Vineyards previously had been sourcing grapes. Charlie and Emily's purchase of Catoctin was not a land purchase but, rather, a purchase of equipment and inventory. Charlie and Emily moved the winery to downtown Frederick and renamed it Frederick Cellars in 2006. Lyon stayed on as winemaker for the first few years of the business.

Elk Run Vineyards

Carol and Fred Wilson make owning a winery look romantic. Their authenticity and European style draw one in and make one want to stay for a while. The Wilsons are the owners of Elk Run Vineyards and are two of the "original disciples" of the famed Dr. Konstantin Frank of New York. They met Frank at a Virginia wine growers' conference, and Fred worked many of the harvests in the 1970s in Frank's vineyards in New York, learning as much as he could.

Dr. Frank encouraged and taught the Wilsons to graft vines, and graft they did! Over the next two years, they grafted thirty-five thousand vines. The grafting materials came from UC–Davis, a recommendation of Dr. Frank. They began planting these vines on a friend's property on the naval base at Carderock. The idea to start a winery became more attractive, and the Wilsons, along with friend and associate Neill Bassford, began their search.

After two years of searching for a suitable vineyard location by doing soil testing, ensuring proper elevation and finding their minimum of forty acres, they found the Resurvey of Cold Friday, a piece of property in Frederick County. Cold Friday was a land grant given to Lord Baltimore from the King of England in the early 1700s.

The winery was bonded in 1983 and has received many high awards from national and international wine competitions. Its first year open, Elk Run was featured in a full-page article in the *Washington Times* Travel Section.

The writer loved the winery's first vintage, and his article moved so much of the wine that Elk Run Vineyards was sold out by Christmas. That was a monumental moment for the winery. Another historic moment for the winery was in 1987, when it took a silver medal in the Beverage Tasting Institute Competition. It was the first winery east of the Rockies to be awarded a silver medal. Elk Run Vineyards has also pioneered certain grape varieties like Malbec, Gewürztraminer and Pinot Noir—all of which have been well received by the public and the trade. Neil Bassford and Bob Cecil, another associate of the winery, have spent many years working in the vineyards and at the winery and teach wine classes both at the winery and off-site.

When Ham Mowbray, owner of Montbray Cellars, decided to sell his winery, Elk Run Vineyards managed the vineyard from 1992 until 1998. The Wilsons made a wine from his Cabernet Sauvignon that was called Mowbray's Cabernet.

LOEW VINEYARDS

Lois and Bill Loew established Loew Vineyards in 1985. Bill has winemaking in his blood, as his family began making honey wine in Galicia, a part of Europe in the Austro-Hungarian Empire, in the 1800s and continued on until World War II began. Bill Loew moved to America and began a profession as an engineer. After meeting Lois, they married, had three daughters and eventually settled in Maryland. Interested in renewing the family tradition of winemaking, they purchased a thirty-seven-acre farm in Frederick County. In 1982, the Loews planted their first acre of grapes, some of which came from Boordy Nursery, and opened the winery three years later just a few miles down the road from Elk Run Vineyard. The vineyard, which sits on rolling hills of gravelly soil, was first planted in 1982 and was a bit of an experimental vineyard. It included varieties like Marechal Foch, Leon Millot, Seyval Blanc, Chancellor, Chardonnay and Riesling. More grape varieties were planted later, like Cabernet Sauvignon, Cabernet Franc and Reliance—an aromatic white wine grape, which makes a wine that the Loews call Serendipity.

The Loews were very active in the formation of Association of Maryland Wineries events and progression, and Lois acted as secretary for several years. Loew Vineyards is also a founding member of the Frederick Wine Trail. They continue to take great pleasure in the arts of grape growing and winemaking.

FIORE WINERY AND DISTILLERY

"I never want to see another grapevine as long as I live!" These were the parting words of a teenage Mike Fiore as his ship set sail from Italy in May 1962. The Maryland wine industry is lucky he didn't stick to his promise.

Fiore grew up in Lamezia Terme in southern Italy, where generations of the Fiore family managed vineyards. During Fiore's adolescence, the Italian government began paying grape farmers to pull out their vineyards and plant olive trees. Not able to understand what had happened to his family legacy, Fiore decided to venture out and went to Naples. From there, he made a decision to move to America.

Fiore left Italy as a seventeen-year-old and arrived in America a short boat ride later. He hopped on a train to Boston and called an old friend from Italy, who helped him find a job and a place to live. It was then that Mike met the second character of this story, his lovely wife, Rose, also an Italian in America. A mere high school graduate when they married, Rose and Mike lived in Boston until 1968.

Mike and Rose moved back and forth to Italy and eventually settled in Maryland in 1971, when Mike worked for Baltimore Gas & Electric. In 1975, they bought a farm in Pylesville, Maryland. It was here that Mike planted some vines for his own personal winemaking, and as the story goes, he outgrew his hobby.

Mike met Ham Mowbray, and in his usual manner, Mowbray encouraged Mike to plant more grapes. Mike tells the story of a wonderful garnet wine that Mowbray made—the only red wine that Rose ever liked. While Mike was planning on planting Vidal Blanc, Mowbray encouraged him to plant Seyval, and in went one thousand vines. Then came six hundred Cabernet Sauvignon vines. Mike finally got to plant his Vidal Blanc and planted three thousand vines. This was the Fiores' La Felicetta Vineyard, the same name as Mike's family vineyard in Italy.

With his now large vineyard, Mike had an excess of grapes. He sold these grapes to bonded wineries, including Boordy Vineyards. Mike was involved in the Maryland Grape Growers Association, and in 1986, Fiore Winery was bonded. Fiore Winery initially produced just 1,500 gallons of wine a year.

In 1998, Mike left his job at BG&E and worked on the winery full time. He revitalized the vineyard, pulling out the Seyval and replacing it with Cabernet Franc. Where there once was Chancellor, now there is Sangiovese, and now Cabernet Sauvignon stands where the Vidal Blanc once was.

Today, Fiore Winery's most produced wine is Cabernet Sauvignon, followed by Chambourcin.

In 2005, due to the passage of legislation, Fiore Winery took the lead in the distillery business in Maryland. It now distills pomace brandy, which is used for both lemoncillo—Rose's family recipe—as well as grappa. Mike's grandson Tony is now helping at the vineyard, learning the winemaking process just as Mike learned from his grandfather. In 2010, Tony made his first wine—a beautiful, off-dry Vignoles. Fiore Winery and Distillery has brought an international legacy, award-winning wines and a whole lot of character to the Maryland wine industry over the past twenty-five years.

Basignani Winery

Basignani Winery is a rustic winery tucked away in the rolling horse country of Baltimore County. Looking at the décor and ambiance of the tasting room, it is immediately apparent that the owners have Italian roots.

Owner Bert Basignani's grandparents always made wine at home, so it was a natural fit for him to continue the tradition. He began his own home winemaking in 1973, when he and his cousin, Albert, made wine in their garage. His then girlfriend (now wife), Lynne, can remember handpicking the grapes off the bunches. "I didn't know you weren't supposed to ferment white wine without the skins," said Basignani about the first wine he made. "The wine was okay." The next year, Bert tried making his wine with local fruit, but it wasn't as ripe as he wanted. So he planted his own grapes in the spring of 1974.

The Basignani's got their grapevines from Philip Wagner, where most grapes were sourced at that point in time. Bert planted sixty vines, all hybrids. Not too long after, Bert's dentist, Eli Shulman, a fellow home winemaker, made an important introduction. He introduced Bert Basignani to Ham Mowbray. Ham encouraged Bert to make another order for grapevines, especially SV-5276, also known as Seyval.

Bert joined the American Wine Society and spent a lot of time learning from Ham Mowbray. He describes Ham as forthcoming with advice. Bert wanted to learn, and Mowbray wanted to teach. "He was inspirational. He had a great palate and taught winemaking courses," said Bert. "He took his classes very seriously, and he inspired me to taste widely. You have to experience really good wines and look outward. Ham took a different approach…to him, wines were a natural product, and quality wines could come from quality fruit."

Bert also had a friendship with Robert Parker, the famed wine critic and creator of the *Wine Advocate*. Parker invited Bert to tastings and introduced him to fine wines: Sauternes, vintage ports, German wines, first-growth Bordeaux—wines Bert wouldn't have tried before.

The Basignani's continued to grow their grapes, originally for their own personal winemaking. They began to realize that they had more than they needed, so they started selling to recently bonded wineries like Woodhall Wine Cellars and Elk Run Vineyards. Bert reflected on his relationship with Al Copp, owner of Woodhall, saying, "He would help me any way he could. Once we were a licensed winery, I can remember sitting down in front of Al before our first Maryland Wine Festival, in 1987. Al told us everything we should take and how to be best prepared."

The Basignani's outgrew their habit of home winemaking and decided to open a commercial winery in 1986. They had a small tasting area filled with inventory that was part-tasting room, part warehouse. They started their business selling four wines: Cabernet Sauvignon, Chardonnay, Marissa (a dry red wine named after their daughter) and Seyval—evidence of Ham Mowbray's influence.

The Basignani's were founding members of the Maryland Grape Growers Association and also the Association of Maryland Wineries. Their humble beginnings have grown to support over ten different wines and three paid staff. Bert and Lynne are known for their Italian-style wines, salt-of-the-earth attitude and consistent leadership in the industry. While Bert may have started as the "new kid on the block," he, too, has provided much guidance and advice to fledgling wineries in the spirit of Ham Mowbray.

A few years after Mowbray's winery, Montbray Cellars, closed, Bert took on management of the old Seyval vineyard. Basignani Winery makes a Montbray Seyval to this day, made from grapes grown in the original Montbray SV-5276 vineyard.

Chapter 5
The Industry Organizes

THE MARYLAND GRAPE GROWERS ASSOCIATION

In Maryland in April 1981, there were seven commercial wineries and a multitude of grape growers, both commercial and hobby growers. In that month, the Maryland Department of Agriculture and the University of Maryland Horticulture Department sponsored a conference for these grape growers. The keynote speaker at the conference was Lucie Morton, one of the East Coast's most prominent vineyard experts.

This first conference had one hundred attendees. A number of these attendees met the next month at Provenza Vineyard and decided to create an organization made up of three committees, based on the group's needs. These groups were research and education; communications; and government affairs/bylaws/nominations. This organization called itself the Maryland Grape Growers Association and was a central location for grape growers to share information about vineyard management and grape growing.

The group met again a month later at Montbray Wine Cellars. By this point, the members had plans for a monthly newsletter, which was called the *Maryland Grapevine*. Judy Wolfe, who eventually became part owner of Catoctin Vineyards with her husband, Roger, was the founding editor. Today, the *Maryland Grapevine* is edited by vineyard owners Emily and Jack Johnston. This publication became a credible tool and was placed in libraries and used by other states.

In addition to creating the *Maryland Grapevine*, MGGA created a set of bylaws and nominated the first officers, with one regulation: no officer of MGGA would be nominated if he or she had a financial interest in a commercial winery, even though many of the original officers would later move on to own wineries.

Al Copp, who didn't open Woodhall Wine Cellars until 1983, was the first president. At that point, he had six acres of grapes planted in Baltimore County. The vice-president was Roger Wolfe, and Jerry Milne was the treasurer. Between Wolfe and Milne, they had twenty-four acres divided evenly between Washington and Frederick Counties. The first treasurer of MGGA was Ed Makosky, who had fifteen acres of grapes in Frederick County.

When the MGGA was formed, there were 116 members. Half of the grapevines were in nine vineyards, with the rest divided among the rest of the members. MGGA also was host to members from out of state, including Pennsylvania, Virginia and West Virginia.

In the late 1980s, MGGA created a Merit Award in memorial of one of the association's members, Woodhall Wine Cellars partner Mike DeSimone, who had an untimely death. The award was granted to members who contributed to grape growing in Maryland to a sufficient degree. Winners of this award over the years have included Paul Steiner, Al Copp, Anne Milne, John McGrew, James and Catherine Russell, Gerald L. Jubb, Carol and Joe Stiepler, Chris Walsh, Fritz Bowers, Jim and Jeanne Moulton, Norb Wagner Jr., George Mead, Bill Kirby, Bob Jennings, Jack and Emily Johnston, Ray Brasfield and Steve Purvins.

John McGrew, one of the early Mike DeSimone Merit Award winners, had a tremendous impact on the grape growers of Maryland through his own research and support. McGrew started as a graduate student at the University of Maryland, researching viruses in strawberries. He did his dissertation on tobacco hybrids and later got a job with the United States Department of Agriculture at the research center in Beltsville, where his focus switched back to strawberry viruses. Coincidentally, McGrew's time in Beltsville was spent at the same agricultural research center where the doomed "New Deal winery" was built. During the 1950s and 1960s, the USDA had a grape program at the Beltsville Research Center, and McGrew got involved. Their research was on black rot, a prominent vineyard disease. In addition to managing the vineyard study, McGrew also planted his own home vineyards in Glenn Dale in the mid-1950s, including grape varieties like Fedonia, Seyval, Chambourcin, Chelois,

Baco and St. Francis. McGrew was a regular contributor to the *Maryland Grapevine* and often spoke at MGGA annual meetings and seminars. He was a true asset and historian to the grape-growing community.

Two of the state's most prominent grape growers are Jack and Emily Johnston. Their vineyard, called Copernica Vineyard, is located not far from where Ham Mowbray's Montbray Cellars was, in Carroll County. Copernica is known for its incredible vinifera grapes, including Cabernet Sauvignon and Cabernet Franc. Woodhall Wine Cellars was one of the Johnstons' clients, and

Copernica Vineyard owner Jack Johnston speaking at an educational seminar at one of the early Maryland Wine Festivals. *Courtesy of Leslie A. Hubbard.*

its award-winning Copernica Reserve Cabernet was sourced from the Johnstons' vineyard.

THE ASSOCIATION OF MARYLAND WINERIES

In 1984, the nine wineries of Maryland began to look for a new outlet to market their product. At this point, most of them were working only out of their tasting rooms and selling their product to select retailers and restaurants. They felt that marketing their products at an event in a central location would offer a new attraction to customers, so they planned the Maryland Wine Festival, a gathering of wineries, wine drinkers and food and craft vendors.

The first Maryland Wine Festival took place at the Union Mills Homestead in Westminster, Maryland, just a few miles from Silver Run, the location of Montbray Wine Cellars. Unlike the large tents that wineries inhabit at today's wine festivals, in 1984, wineries used just a few tables to showcase their products. Winery owners remember customers pulling wagons of wine out of the event because, at that point, local wine was less readily available at local wine shops.

The Maryland Wine Festival created a need for a unified group to sign the event's first contract. The wineries formed the Association of Maryland

Above: Phyllis Mowbray offering author Leon Adams a bottle of Montbray Wine Cellars recent vintage at one of the first Maryland Wine Festivals. *Courtesy of Leslie A. Hubbard.*

Left: Ham Mowbray and Rob Deford at the Maryland Wine Festival. *©Estate of Hamilton Mowbray. Used by permission.*

Mike and Helle DeSimone, former owners of Woodhall Wine Cellars, at one of the first Maryland Wine Festivals. *Courtesy of Leslie A. Hubbard.*

Wineries, which would help guide the industry through the next decades of growth and challenges. The next year, with more wineries on board, the festival moved to the Carroll County Farm Museum.

The Maryland Wine Festival has grown to host upward of forty wineries and nearly thirty thousand guests annually. Similar groups around the state have modeled after this festival, and it has been duplicated in surrounding states.

The AMW began because the wineries needed an organization to sign a contract with Carroll County. The goals of the association grew to include collaboratively marketing and promoting the wineries of Maryland both through and outside of the Maryland Wine Festival. The MGGA was already in action, providing information on grape growing and winemaking for everyone from the hobbyist to the commercial vineyard or winery. The AMW was the second extension of that effort in marketing the final product. While some members of the MGGA were hesitant about the formation of a new winery group because they thought it would divide the industry and the MGGA might lose members, there was a need for a new association that met the specific needs of commercial wineries.

The first president of the Association of Maryland Wineries was Rob Deford of Boordy Vineyards. The AMW did more than provide an opportunity for a festival. It also offered a new opportunity for commercial wineries to gather to exchange ideas and experiences and unite their marketing efforts. Al Copp, founding member of the MGGA, noted the value of the formation of the AMW, saying, "Wineries had a camaraderie. We shared everything—corks, secrets and the market."

PROFESSIONALIZATION OF THE ASSOCIATION

In 1999, the association decided to hire a public relations firm, Baltimore-based Himmelrich, to aid in marketing and publicizing the industry. In 2002, the Association of Maryland Wineries, under the guidance of Himmelrich, received a Specialty Crop Grant to fund a marketing campaign called "Ask for Maryland Wine" to support the eleven wineries in the state. Market share was only .85 percent of all wine consumed in Maryland. The goals of the campaign were to increase the market share, increase demand for the product, offer incentive to potential grape growers to plant vineyards and enhance the promotion of the state hospitality and tourism industries. The grant resulted in the "Ask for Maryland Wine" logo and tagline, as well as display stickers and point of sale materials for restaurants and wine shops.

After a few years, the PR firm encouraged the AMW to hire someone to manage the membership, legislation, events, marketing and strategic planning of the industry and association—an executive director. Himmelrich led the association through a hiring process that yielded the organization's first staff member, a young man named Kevin Atticks who contracted with Himmelrich. Kevin was familiar to the wineries because of his 1999 book, *Discovering Maryland Wineries*, the first of a series of travel guides to regional wineries. Atticks held a master's degree in environmental journalism and was a professor at Loyola College, where he taught journalism, public relations and visual communications.

Atticks soon became a key player in the industry's development. In 2003, he completed his doctorate in communications design and took over the association's public relations and management functions. One of Atticks's first proposals was to change the name of the organization from Association of Maryland Wineries to Maryland Wineries Association (MWA), a minor change but one that brought the organization on par with other statewide trade groups.

Over time, Atticks established an office in Timonium, all the while ushering more wineries into the industry. Despite being a self-proclaimed introvert, Atticks has artfully created a network of relationships, from the agricultural community to the tourism community, from state legislators to wine shop owners and media and press. This carefully strategized spider web of networks created a safety net of connections for the association and the industry as a whole. Atticks became a resource for industry and non-industry requests alike.

The Maryland Wineries Association, unlike many of its peer organizations in neighboring states, is almost entirely self-funded. Since 2009, the MWA has hired two additional full-time staff members, as well as a rotating team of interns each semester. This staff aids the executive director and the board in planning and executing marketing, legislative and promotional programs and events.

The MWA offers many benefits to its members and remains one of the only state associations to boast 100 percent membership—every single licensed winery in the state of Maryland is a member of MWA. It could be due to its low annual dues, but more likely it's due to the plethora of member benefits that the organization offers.

The MWA is guided by a board of directors broken up into committees. These committees do the work of the association and determine what direction the industry should take. The committees then make recommendations to the board, which then instructs the association staff to execute those recommendations. This dictates the staff responsibilities, which include offering legislative guidance, lobbying and strategic lawmaking for the industry; creating marketing programs, including a comprehensive website, social networking campaign, restaurant and wine shop incentive programs; wine trail programs; and winery visitation tools. True to its roots of organizing events and marketing programs, the association continues this tradition, introducing new and different events and marketing programs each year.

A decade after he was hired, Atticks still serves as executive director and has ushered more than forty commercial wineries into business. He continues to shepherd interested parties into the industry, warning them of the risks, the investment and the hard work that is required to be a successful local winery. The hiring of an executive director is noted as a monumental moment to the industry, according to many wineries. In the words of Rob Deford, "Kevin was young and had promise."

THE OTHER FESTIVALS

The second flagship wine festival sponsored by the MWA is called Wine in the Woods. This event is hosted by Howard County Parks and Recreation. The festival has historically taken place in a park called Symphony Woods, located right next to the famed concert venue Merriweather Post Pavilion. The festival started in 1992 and draws crowds as large as the Maryland Wine Festival.

The Autumn Wine Festival is hosted by Wicomico Tourism and takes place at Pemberton Park in Salisbury. It is a smaller festival, usually drawing fewer than five thousand people. About the same size, the Riverside Wine Festival takes place at Historic Sotterley in Hollywood. Both of these events take place in October of each year.

The Easterns Bayside Blues and Wine Fest is hosted by the Eastern Yacht Club in Essex, Maryland. Great Grapes: Cockeysville is run by the Trigger Agency and is located at Oregon Ridge. Each of these events draws several thousand people.

Most recently, the Maryland Wineries Association has launched its own independent events, including Decanter, the first ever MWA-run Baltimore city wine festival, which takes place at Pimlico Race Course, home of the Preakness. MWA has also launched a series of new events called Eat•Drink•Go LOCAL, which are farmers' market–style events, bringing together restaurants, wineries and farmers from certain regions to downtown areas.

THE TURN-OF-THE-MILLENNIUM WINERIES

After the MWA was formed, three wineries—Loew Vineyards, Fiore Winery and Basignani Winery—opened. For ten years thereafter, there was no growth in the number of wineries, until 1996.

The first winery to open in Carroll County after Montbray Vineyards was Cygnus Wine Cellars. Owner Ray Brasfield opened the winery in 1996 after leaving his post as winemaker at Woodhall Wine Cellars. Cygnus Wine Cellars is located in historic Manchester. The winery's estate vineyard is located just a few miles away at Brasfield's residence. Brasfield's wines are European in style, with food-friendly red wines and aromatic white wines. Cygnus Wine Cellars is best known for its Julian label Cabernet Sauvignon and méthode champenoise sparkling wines. Brasfield was the well-respected president of the Maryland Wineries Association from 2008 to 2012. He provided much to the industry in terms of focus, balance of views and leadership during those years.

In the far reaches of Maryland's left extension lies Garrett County, home of Deep Creek Cellars, owned by Paul Roberts and Nadine Grabiana. Opened in 1997, Deep Creek Cellars is a cottage-style winery, making low-production, European-style wines. The winery is at 2,100 feet elevation atop a south-facing hill. Roberts, a former president of the Maryland Wineries Association, practices sustainable vineyard management. Like Bob Lyon of Catoctin Vineyards, Paul spent a year as an apprentice at Chateau Montelana, where he learned how to make wine. Deep Creek Cellars produces mostly dry, rustic wines. Paul practices sustainable farming methods and uses efficient winemaking techniques, like a gravity-flow bottling system.

In 2000, Jan and Maura Luigard bonded Penn Oaks Winery in Silver Spring. Jan Luigard was inspired by his many worldwide travels, which created an affinity for the Germanic-style wines that Penn Oaks Winery now produces. Jan has built a winery and planted a vineyard at a site in Howard County, where he hopes to move the winery in the future

Little Ashby, owned by Warren and Lynne Rich, was the first winery to open on the Eastern Shore. Rich grows Bordeaux variety gapes and creates incredible "Super Tuscans," age-worthy ports and structured red wines and Chardonnays. Located on the banks of the Miles River in Talbot County, the winery is situated close to the towns of Easton and St. Michaels. Dogs are always welcome at Little Ashby, as is reflected on each of its labels—a sketch of owner and winemaker Warren Rich's own Labradors. Lynne passed away in 2011 and is a missed member of the local wine industry.

Chapter 6
The Second Growth

At the turn of the millennium, the industry boomed. Growth skyrocketed due to a variety of factors. Part of the growth was due to the professionalization of the Association of Maryland Wineries and the hiring of an executive director in 2002. The newly hired executive director, Kevin Atticks, played many roles in the association, including aiding in industry and winery marketing and public relations, legislative action and especially in county zoning and winery licensing processes.

A precedent was—and is—set each time a county licensed its first winery. The rules that the county created and enforced for that new winery would carry over to every winery that opened thereafter. The culmination of experience and knowledge garnered by MWA made this process more efficient and set a benchmark for other counties to recognize.

An organized association continued to provide an opportunity for wineries and other industry members to gather to share ideas, thoughts and resources. The association was a bank of knowledge for individuals interested in starting a winery and may have been one of the key factors in the upward growth of wineries and vineyards in the state.

Each region of the state has its own story of growth. Some counties and regions grew quickly because of enthused regulators and legislators, while others were slow to start.

A Full-Bodied History

Southern Maryland

Southern Maryland is dotted with old red tobacco barns, open fields and various waterways. The region is one of Maryland's most historic, and its crop had always been tobacco. Until 2004, there were twelve active wineries in Maryland, none of which was located in the southern part of the state until three new wineries began. The first licensed winery in southern Maryland is called Cove Point Winery and is named after the state's oldest operational lighthouse. The winery is owned by Tim and Sheryl Lewis. Cove Point has kept its charm after moving into a new tasting room in front of the winemaking facility. The small vineyard at Cove Point Winery includes a number of grapes, including Cayuga White, Chardonnel, Neptune, Dornfelder and many other varieties not often found in Maryland vineyards.

Around the same time, Ken and Ann Korando opened two wineries: Chapel Cellars in Historic St. Mary's City and Solomons Island Winery. Chapel Cellars was a collaboration with Historic St. Mary's City, a combination of historic property and winery. It was licensed and located in the basement of Farthing's Ordinary, a general store. The winery faced difficulties because of its location on historic property and had to close in 2006. Around the same time that they opened Chapel Cellars, the Korandos opened Solomons Island Winery in Solomons Island, Calvert County, which has become one of Maryland's most popular festival wineries, producing a line of fruit- and grape-based wines, as well as a line of dry wines. Korando has a winery project in New Zealand, where he spends some of his time during Maryland's slower seasons.

Fridays Creek Winery, owned by the Cleary family, opened for business in 2006. This multi-generational winery is built with the expertise of this family of farmers, homebuilders and firefighters. The winery is set in a historic tobacco barn in Owings, Calvert County. It produces a variety of wines, from hybrid and vinifera varietals to blends and fruit wines.

In Calvert County, along the Patuxent Wine Trail, lies a town called St. Leonard. It was here, on this farm, situated between the Chesapeake Bay and the Patuxent River, that owners John Behun and Mark Flemming planted 2,200 vinifera vines in 2002. Five years later, they opened Perigeaux Vineyards and Winery. The vineyard has since grown to eight acres of almost 5,000 vines. This winery is also entirely estate vineyard supported, consisting of eight acres of vinifera varieties.

Perhaps considered a bit north of southern Maryland, Heimbuch Estate Vineyards and Winery was the first winery to open in Anne Arundel County, producing wines under the "Thanksgiving Farm" moniker. Opened in 2006 by Doug and Maureen Heimbuch, the winery uses only grapes grown on their own property. Doug and Maureen live on a historic property called Thanksgiving Farm, which is made up of about fifty-eight acres historically used as tobacco fields. After realizing that the terroir, the temperature and the growing season might make for excellent wine, they expanded their operation. The Heimbuchs focus all their winemaking efforts on creating a Meritage blend, a Pommeroll-style wine that is their pride and joy. The winery will occasionally produce a lighter red or a dry rosé when the vintage allows it. It was the first winery to open in Anne Arundel County, only a few miles from the state capital. Just a few years later, two other wineries—the Vineyards at Dodon and Great Frogs at Harness Creek Vineyards—have begun to put down roots.

In 2000, Mike Scarborough purchased a three-hundred-acre farm in Prince Frederick for hunting purposes. After realizing that the land might be suitable for grape growing, Scarborough planted about one hundred vines in 2002. The winery opened in 2008, and like Perigeaux Vineyards and Winery, it has grown to about eight acres. Soon after the winery opened, Mike and his wife, Barb, built a large event venue resembling a Tuscan villa. Mike and Barb have big dreams for this wine destination. Running Hare produces a variety of wines, including hybrids and vinifera. It has produced award-winning dessert wines made from the Chambourcin grape, among many, many other varieties and styles like Chardonnay, Malbec and more.

As wineries in Calvert County opened, St. Mary's County, just south of Calvert, became home to several grape growers. Not having enough grapes to start their own wineries, this group of growers organized to become the Southern Maryland Grape Growers Cooperative (SMGGC). This co-op, with the help of the county, formed Port of Leonardtown Winery in 2010. Port of Leonardtown Winery was the first winery in St. Mary's County. Each of the grape growers on the board of the SMGGC contributes grapes at harvest. The vineyards that contribute to Port of Leonardtown Winery are Long Looked For, Come at Last Vineyard; Gemeny Farms; Gossett Farm; Purvins Farm Vineyard; St. Michaels Manor Vineyard; Summerseat Farm Vineyard; Waterford Vineyard; Wishful Thinking Farm; Piney Grove Vineyard; and Forrest Hall Farms. These vineyards' grapes are combined and used to make wines for the Port of Leonardtown Winery. They have had many successes so far, and their wines, made by winemaker Pat Isles, are standing out in the mix of other local wines.

Slack Winery was the second winery to open in St. Mary's County. Owned by Maggie O'Brien, Jim Grube and their son, Tucker Grube-O'Brien, Slack opened in 2010. The twenty-acre vineyard and winery are located at Jubilee Farm in Leonardtown, while the tasting room resides at the historic Woodlawn Farm estate and bed-and-breakfast in Ridge. Jubilee Farm was planted with four thousand vines in 2002 and included traditional vinifera varieties but also more unusual Italian varietals like Montepulciano and Barbera. In 2009, white grapes like Albariño and Chardonnay were added to the vineyard. The farm and vineyard originally supplied other wineries like Woodhall Wine Cellars, but now all the grapes grown on the farm are used in Slack wines. Woodlawn Farm, where the tasting room is located, is home to a 1789 English manor home and boxwood gardens. Woodlawn Farm is located in Ridge, Maryland. Slack wines take on a no-nonsense approach, not fitting within one style or criteria but, rather, representing the vineyard successes of the year in each bottle.

Golden Leaf Farm, home to the Romano Vineyards and Winery, was the first winery in Prince George's County. The winery, owned by Joe and Jo-Ann Romano opened in 2011. In addition to growing grapes, Golden Leaf Farm was first home to many honeybees. Joe and Jo-Ann have been collecting honey since 1998. In 2007, the Romanos decided to plant grapes in what used to be corn, soybean and tobacco fields. Joe is the winemaker and Jo-Ann the vineyard manager.

While southern Maryland did not bloom as a winery region until after the millennium, it proves to be a region with much potential. The growing conditions are ideal for certain varieties of grapes, and the future is looking very optimistic. Especially helpful is the supportive tourism industry, which has encouraged the Patuxent Wine Trail, of which many of these southern Maryland wineries are part.

THE EASTERN SHORE

The Eastern Shore, one of Maryland's largest regions, stretches from the Upper Shore to Ocean City, Maryland. With a rich agricultural history steeped in corn and seafood farming, the Eastern Shore is rich, abundant farmland. Many grape growers in Maryland didn't believe that the Eastern Shore was suitable for growing grapes, especially vinifera varieties. Bill Kirby disagreed. Kirby planted the first vinifera on the Eastern Shore in 1983 in Wye Mills, located in Cordova, in upper Talbot County. His vineyard consisted of both vinifera and hybrids. It was previously said that vinifera could only grow at an elevation of six hundred miles above sea level, so this was a big first attempt.

In 1995, Bill planted three more vinifera varieties, which he hoped would be turned into a Bordeaux blend, Cabernet Sauvignon, Merlot and Cabernet Franc. Bill's grapes were sold to Boordy Vineyards for some time and later were purchased by Woodhall Wine Cellars. Bill also sold grapes to Fred Wilson at Elk Run Vineyards, and now his vineyard supplies St. Michaels Winery, owned by Mark Emon, Lori Cuthbert and Seth and Allison Jones.

Tilmon's Island Winery is not located on the Eastern Shore's Tilghman Island but, rather, is located just north of Sudlersville in Queen Anne's County on the Eastern Shore. This winery was opened in 2005 by Don Tilmon and certainly meets the definition of a boutique winery, with very small production of about five hundred cases annually. Tilmon's Island Winery sources grapes from local counties, including Caroline, Talbot and Queen Anne's.

The Eastern Shore's largest winery, St. Michaels Winery, is named for the small seaside destination town where it is located. It opened in 2005. This winery sources from vineyards throughout Maryland, including Bill Kirby's, as well as other vineyards it owns on the shore. It is well known for its nautical-themed labels and tasting room and its "Gollywobbler" series, named after a staysail on a sailboat. Most recently, St. Michaels has made a Bordeaux blend from Bill Kirby's beloved vinifera vineyard—one of Kirby's long-term goals achieved.

Cascia Vineyards is situated just over the Chesapeake Bay Bridge on Kent Island, a small island that divides Annapolis from the Eastern Shore. This winery, owned by Mark and Kim Cascia, was licensed in 2006. Mark and Kim have twelve acres of grapes planted. While they have yet to open to the public, their wines are available at regional festivals and are making their mark. They have planted and are making wines with new varieties to Maryland, like Orange Muscat.

Terrapin Station Winery, owned by Morris and Janet Zwick, is currently maker of the only boxed wine in the state and opened in 2006. Located on the Upper Shore, in Cecil County, the winery and vineyard sit on the farm of Janet's family home. Like many of Maryland's old farm families, Janet's family needed to make a decision about the future of the farm. Their options were either to sell the property to developers or use the land and make it sustainable. Janet and Morris decided to plant grapes in 2003. The owners, both University of Maryland alumni, are devoted to their alma mater's mascot, the terrapin. A percentage from each box sold goes to the Terrapin Institute, a group dedicated to saving the Maryland state reptile. Terrapin Station Winery takes pride in making wine fun and approachable.

Cassinelli Vineyards and Winery, owned by Al and Jennifer Cassinelli, is located on a 110-acre farm in Churchville, Maryland. Al, an investment banker and retired U.S. Marine, opened the winery in 2007. On the farm, guests may meet their friendly retrievers, as well as their twenty-five Black Angus cows, five buffalo and two donkeys. In addition to Chardonnay, Merlot and Viognier grapes, the farm is home to hundreds of peach, apple, pear and plum trees.

Bordeleau Vineyards and Winery, owned by Tom Shelton, opened in 2007. Shelton worked at the Perdue Chicken Company for many years and eventually made his way up in the company to the position of president. Upon retirement in 1986, Tom started his own poultry company called Case Farms. In 1999, he decided to plant vines at his farm in Eden, Maryland. Bordeleau was the first licensed winery in Wicomico County. The name Bordeleau means "edge of the water" and is quite appropriate, as the vineyard, winery and gorgeous home sit on Wicomico Creek, a tributary of the Chesapeake Bay. Shelton has ten varieties of grapes on ten acres of land. He focuses on Bordeaux varieties and has received recognition for his quality of wines.

Dove Valley Winery, owned by Harry Hepbron and the Hepbron family, opened in 2007. It is the second winery to open in Cecil County. The Hepbron's grow mostly vinifera and have had great success with an grape unusual to Maryland, called Vignoles.

Far Eastern Shore Winery was licensed in 2008 and is owned by Tien-Seng and Tara Chiu. Their focus is on grape-based wines with different fruit components.

Layton's Chance Vineyard and Winery opened in 2010 in Dorchester County. The Laytons are a fourth-generation farming family. After years of growing grain and other crops, the family looked for another way to diversify the family farm. Grapes were the way to go for the Laytons, and now they have a bustling farm winery. The Layton family was inducted into the Maryland Department of Agriculture Hall of Fame in 2011.

Costa Ventosa Vineyard and Winery, Italian for "windy coast," is the closest winery to Ocean City—one of the state's biggest tourism destinations. Owned by Kathryn Danko-Lord and Jack Lord, Costa Ventosa consists of ten acres of vineyard and farmland in Whaleyville, Worcester County. The site's first vines were planted in 2006, and the winery opened in 2010. Kathryn and Jack take a lighthearted, fun approach to their winery. Guests can always expect to have a good time and a laugh—and some tasty wines, as well!

Great Shoals Winery was the second winery to specialize in apple wines, opening in 2011. Owner Matt Cimino took a different approach, crafting naturally fermenting champagne-style wines. Aside from apple, Great Shoals Winery also produces wines made from pear, peach and grapes. One of these first wines was even made with pomegranates grown on his property on the Eastern Shore. Matt's training is in forensic botany, so winemaking was a drastic, but welcome, change.

Soon to be joining the Eastern Shore region is Crow Vineyard and Winery, also a B&B in Kennedyville.

FREDERICK COUNTY

Frederick County is home to historic vineyards and wineries. With such existing vineyards as Linganore Winecellars, Elk Run Vineyards, Loew Vineyards and Catoctin Vineyards, it was just a matter of time before new wineries put down their roots.

Black Ankle Vineyards was the next winery to open in 2005. When owners Ed Boyce and Sarah O'Herron decided to leave their consulting jobs, they took a look at what they wanted to do with their knowledge, time and efforts and decided to open a winery. Ed and Sarah looked all over the East Coast for the perfect site and found a farm on Black Ankle Road in Mount Airy. Twenty-two acres of grapes were planted over 2003 and 2004. In 2010, twenty more acres were planted. The varieties include Albariño, Cabernet Franc, Cabernet Sauvignon, Grüner Veltliner, Malbec, Merlot, Petit Verdot, Pinot Noir, Syrah and Viognier. Black Ankle was named one of the country's "hottest small brands" by *Wine Business Monthly* in 2011. Black Ankle Vineyards has been noted as one of the game-changing wineries in the state. It has done things differently than many of the other wineries, for example, practicing tight row placement in the vineyard and making only dry wines.

Sugarloaf Mountain Vineyard, like Black Ankle Vineyards, came out of the gate with some incredibly grown and made wines. The original ninety-two-acre farm, located at the base of Sugarloaf Mountain, was purchased by Dan and Polly O'Donohugh in 1962. Dan and Polly's four children, the McGarry, McKenna and two O'Donohugh families, turned this family retreat into a vineyard and now winery. While the winery is located in Montgomery County, it was adopted into the Frederick Wine Trail because

The tasting room located in the barn at Sugarloaf Mountain Vineyards. *Courtesy of Sugarloaf Mountain Vineyard, photographer Richard Cress.*

of its proximity to the Frederick County line. Some of Sugarloaf Mountain Vineyard's grape acreage also lies within Frederick County. The winery produces mostly dry varietal wines. Red blends, rosés and white varietals make up most of the portfolio, with an occasional off dry or desert wine to be spotted.

Charlie Daneri and Emily Williams were ready to look for some land to settle down on after their children were grown and had gone away to college. They had met Bob Lyon, owner and winemaker at Catoctin Vineyard, and told him what they were looking for. Bob directed them to a piece of property in Middletown. On the property was a two-acre vineyard planted by the property's previous owners, three doctors who sold their grapes to Catoctin Vineyards. The vineyard was planted in 1992 with grape cuttings from famed wineries Chateau Montelana, Dunn Vineyards and Silver Oak Cellars of California.

Charlie and Emily learned that Bob Lyon was ready to sell Catoctin Vineyards, so they stepped in and purchased the winery's equipment and wine inventory. They reopened the winery as Frederick Cellars in 2006 and moved it to downtown Frederick. They purchased much of the Catoctin Vineyards' wine reserve to sell from Frederick Cellars and even retained Lyon as a winemaking consultant after Catoctin was sold. Lyon mentored Charlie in the ways of winemaking over the next few years.

Frederick Cellars is housed in an old brick warehouse, formerly the Crystal Ice House, which was built in 1904 in the Everedy Square and Shab Row district in downtown Frederick. One of the original partners for Frederick Cellars was Don Segal, owner of Harness Creek Vineyards in Annapolis. Frederick Cellars used grapes from Harness Creek Vineyards until about 2008, when the two parties split ways. In 2011, Frederick Cellars began sourcing grapes from Antietam Vineyards in Washington County, owned by Richard Penna. Charlie and Emily knew Penna from their time as members of the Maryland Grape Growers Association, with which he was heavily involved. Charlie and Emily leased this vineyard even through Penna's sickness and eventual passing away. Frederick Cellars has carried on some of the traditions of Catoctin Vineyards, like its Eye of the Oriole blush wine and many library Cabernets.

Orchid Cellar was founded in 2006 and was the first winery dedicated to making mead in Maryland. It is owned by Andrzej and Marzanna Wilk, natives of Poland, who have extended their family tradition of making honey wine to the United States. The Wilks' son, Andrzej Jr., acts as assistant winemaker. Orchid Cellar makes a variety of styles of mead, including traditional recipes made with spices and rose petals. One of its biggest sellers is a nontraditional mead called Hunter, made with the addition of hot peppers. It has a balance of sweetness from the honey and heat from the peppers. The meads made by Orchid Cellar are aged in French oak, and the process can take longer than making some regular grape wines—often up to two years. Orchid Cellars' tasting room opened in 2011 in Middletown.

Just a few miles away from Orchid Cellar is another apple wine–focused winery in Frederick County. Distillery Lane Ciderworks was the first of a new set of wineries that specialize in cider-style apple wines. Opened in 2011, Distillery Lane Ciderworks is also home to one of the largest heirloom apple orchards in the state of Maryland, consisting of more than two thousand apple trees of thirty different varieties. Historically, the Miller-Power family sold apples and crafted non-alcoholic ciders, but they decided to branch out and created a farmhouse cider–style wine with the broad varieties of apples they grow on their farm. Each vintage and cider is unique.

Catoctin Breeze Vineyard also opened in 2011 and is located just down the road from Mount St. Mary's University near Emmitsberg, Maryland. Owners Voytek and Alicja Fiztya are making both grape wine and mead. Their vineyard sits on limestone soil near the Catoctin Mountains.

The Piedmont Grows

Baltimore and Harford County are also home to historic vineyards and wineries. Home to John Adlum's Havre de Grace Vineyard and both Philip Wagner and Rob Deford's Boordy Vineyards, this region continued to expand in 2007 with the opening of Mount Felix Vineyard and Winery. This winery pays homage to John Adlum through its wine's names. The owners, Peter and Mary Ianiello, have created a lovely bed-and-breakfast out of their historic home, perfectly accompanied by the on-site winery and vineyard.

Legends Vineyard, located in Churchville, was established in 2005 by owners Ashby and Carrie Everhart. The winery began selling wine in 2008. Ashby acts as winemaker, and Carrie manages the marketing and sales. They are joined by partner Greg O'Hare, who helps with the vineyard. It was Harford County's third winery and makes a broad portfolio of wines.

The next winery to open, named after the county, was Harford Vineyard and Winery in 2009. Kevin and Teresa Mooney began Harford Vineyard as a grape juice and winemaking supply outlet for home winemakers before deciding to open their own winery. The Mooneys planted Vidal and Traminette grapes in 2003 and Merlot in 2005. The winery opened in 2009, and Harford Vineyard became an active member of the Piedmont Wine Trail.

DeJon Vineyards was the fourth winery to open in Baltimore County, after Boordy Vineyards, Woodhall Wine Cellars and Basignani Winery. The winery is located just down the road from Boordy Vineyards, in the Long Green Valley, and was opened in 2010 by John Wilkerson and Denise McCloskey.

Baltimore County's most recent addition is Royal Rabbit Vineyards, owned by Roy and Linda Albin. Located in Parkton, the winery opened for business in November 2011.

Baltimore City joined the ranks of winery-housed districts, as Aliceanna Winery established its roots in the Canton neighborhood of the city in 2011.

Owned by Erik Bandzak, the winery is not currently open to the public but maintains a small production within the city limits—a first for Maryland!

Recently joining the Piedmont region is a winery called Chateau Bonita, and soon to join is Millstone Cellars; both are in Baltimore County.

CARROLL COUNTY REGAINS SPEED

Joining Cygnus Wine Cellars in Carroll County, Galloping Goose Vineyard, which opened in 2008, is the first woman-owned and-operated winery in Maryland. Diane Hale, owner, winemaker and vineyard manager, started first as a commercial grower, producing some of the best fruit in Carroll County. She expanded to make her own wine, selecting from her twenty-seven acres of both vinifera and hybrid grapes. Her winery is named after Goose, her racing horse that used to be a star at Pimlico Race Course, home of the Preakness Stakes. Diane focuses on small-batch, dry vinifera wines.

Serpent Ridge Vineyard was the third winery to open in Carroll County and is owned by Karen and Greg Lambrecht. The winery opened in the spring of 2009 and was named for the abundance of reptiles found on the vineyard site. Serpent Ridge Vineyard was the first winery on the East Coast to use a plastic bottle closure, called a Zork. Greg and Karen take pride in using modern-day technology to replicate Old World–style wines like Cabernet blends and single-varietal white wines. The Lambrechts source grapes from Carroll County vineyards, especially their own.

The two newest additions to the Carroll Wine Trail are Detour Vineyard and Winery in Keymar and Old Westminster Winery in Westminster. Detour Vineyard and Winery is owned by the Tamminga family and opened in December 2011. Old Westminster Winery is owned and operated by the Baker family. Owners Jay and Ginger Baker and their three children run the new family business. Wanting to make their family farm sustainable, the Bakers decided to grow grapes and open a winery. Drew, the oldest child in the family, is the CEO of the winery. Lisa the second oldest, has a degree in chemistry and is the youngest female winemaker in the state. Youngest sister Ashli will direct the marketing efforts of Old Westminster Winery.

WESTERN MARYLAND EXTENDS

Washington County is one of the state's most up-and-coming regions in terms of wine production. Knob Hall Winery opened in 2010 and is owned by Dick and Mary Beth Seibert. Dick's family owned the farm for many generations, and it seemed to be a perfect location for vast vineyards and a winery operation. The barn where the tasting room is situated was built about 1860 using wood and stone from the farm. Knob Hall Winery has thirty acres of estate vineyards, including Cabernet Franc, Cabernet Sauvignon, Chambourcin, Malbec, Merlot, Petit Verdot, Albariño, Chardonnay, Pinot Gris, Traminette, Vidal Blanc and Viognier. One of few female winemakers in Maryland, Mary Beth has released high-quality wines straight out of the gate.

Randy and Jennifer Thompson saw potential in Washington County and invited Dave Collins, former winemaker at the famed Breaux Vineyards in Loudoun County, Virginia, to partner in their new endeavor. Many acres of grapes are in the ground, and the winery will be called Big Cork Vineyards. The Thompsons and Collinses hope to open the winery in 2013.

WINE TRAILS

Wineries clustered around the state have been grouped into wine trails, based loosely off the stated growing regions. Each region has its own identity and variety of attractions.

The Frederick Wine Trail was the first trail to be formed in 2006, through a grant from the Maryland Department of Agriculture. The trail originally included Berrywine Plantation/Linganore Winecellars, Elk Run Vineyards, Frederick Cellars, Loew Vineyards and Black Ankle Vineyards—all the Frederick County wineries. Sugarloaf Mountain Vineyards was also added to the trail. This winery is located in Montgomery County but borders Frederick County and is only a short drive away. As other wineries opened in Frederick County, they were added to the trail. This list includes Orchid Cellar, Distillery Lane Ciderworks and Catoctin Breeze Vineyard.

The second wine trail formed was the Chesapeake Wine Trail, encompassing the wineries of the whole Eastern Shore. The original trail included Dove Valley Winery, Terrapin Station Winery, Cassinelli Winery, Mark Cascia Vineyards, Tilmon's Island Winery, Little Ashby Vineyards,

The vineyard of Catoctin Breeze Vineyards, located in mountainous Frederick County. *Courtesy of Voytek Fiztya.*

St. Michaels Winery and Bordeleau Vineyards and Winery. Layton's Chance Vineyard and Winery, Costa Ventosa Vineyard and Winery and Great Shoals Winery eventually joined the ranks. While this is one of the larger trails, it can be broken up into two regions: the Upper Shore and Lower Shore.

The third wine trail to open was the Piedmont Wine Trail, inclusive of wineries in Baltimore and Harford Counties. Boordy Vineyards, DeJon Vineyards, Fiore Winery, Harford Vineyard and Winery, Mount Felix Vineyard and Winery, Legends Vineyard, Woodhall Wine Cellars and Basignani Winery make up this trail.

The fourth wine trail to launch was the Patuxent Wine Trail, collecting the wineries of southern Maryland, specifically Calvert County, into a group. The Calvert County wineries on the trail are Fridays Creek Winery, Running Hare Vineyards, Cove Point Winery, Solomons Island Winery and Perigeaux Vineyards and Winery. In 2010, two wineries in neighboring St. Mary's County opened, Port of Leonardtown Winery and Slack Winery. These wineries also joined the Patuxent Wine Trail.

A Full-Bodied History

The fifth and most recent wine trail to launch was the Carroll Wine Trail, including Cygnus Wine Cellars, Serpent Ridge Vineyard and Galloping Goose Winery in Carroll County. The future of wine trails in the state will likely include a break-off of smaller trails on the Eastern Shore and a stand-alone trail in the western part of the state. As new wineries open, the trails will adjust and morph into smaller, denser regions.

Chapter 7

The Legislative Efforts
of the Maryland Wine Industry

M ost states' alcohol laws were reconstructed after the repeal of
Prohibition, with the goal of preventing the regrowth of the chaos
of the early twentieth century. Maryland in the 1930s did not have a
vibrant alcohol manufacturing industry, so wineries and breweries were not
given much consideration when the modern alcohol law was created post-
Prohibition. This, plus the recent increase in wine tourism, has changed the
way the public views local wineries.

Maryland's alcohol statutes were built on the concept that it is the state's
role to promote temperance. The Merriam-Webster Dictionary defines
temperance as the "moderation in or abstinence from the use of alcoholic
beverages." In other words, Maryland's alcohol law was designed to keep
alcohol from freely reaching the market.

The State of Maryland follows what is called a three-tier distribution
system for alcohol. This means that there are three tiers of process that
alcohol—a regulated product—must go through before it reaches the
consumer. The first tier is the manufacturer. This is the maker of the
product, for example a distillery, brewery or winery. The second tier in the
system is the wholesaler. This is the party that is legally required to purchase
the product from the manufacturer and is the sole purveyor of the product
to retail outlets. The wholesaler then sells it to the third party, or tier, the
retailer. The retailer is the restaurant or shop that sells the product to the
consumer. In every state, there tend to be many manufacturers and retailers
but many fewer wholesalers. When Prohibition was repealed, the three-

tier system was built to ensure that alcohol was appropriately regulated. Sadly, wineries don't easily fit into this three-tier system, as they are a unique business model that happens to be a manufacturer, a wholesaler and quite often a retailer of its own product.

For quite some time, the state laws were so archaic that they stated a winery could only sell one quart of wine to any one person each year. Each winery's activities were determined by the liquor board in the county where the winery was located. Each of the county liquor boards interpreted laws regarding wineries differently, so not only was there old-fashioned law, but it also changed from county to county.

State excise sales tax stamps. *Courtesy of the Office of the Maryland State Comptroller.*

The state alcohol code, titled Article 2B, as originally written, left no room for the wine industry to develop or become a sustainable business option. Over the past eighty years, the alcohol industry, wineries included, has brought different scenarios and requests to the state legislature to persuade it to improve the alcohol code.

In 1951, a law was passed that allowed Maryland wineries to bypass wholesalers and sell directly to restaurants and retailers.

In 1977, both Linganore Winecellars and Byrd Winery of Frederick County were told by the Alcohol and Trade Division of the state that they could no longer sell wine on Sundays. The wineries turned to George Roche of the Maryland Department of Agriculture for help. From there, a representative from the Maryland Farm Bureau met with the state retailer (wine shop) association to discuss the issue. From this meeting, the wineries learned that retailers were concerned that wineries did not have to "jump through the hoops" that the retailers did in terms of applying and paying for a retail license through the County Liquor Commissioners.

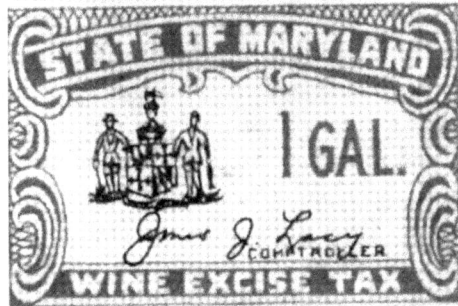

The six wineries of the time gathered and agreed to meet the concerns of the retailers. A bill was constructed and introduced by Senator Ed Thomas in the 1978 session. From this effort came the Class A Light Wine License, which allowed wineries to sell unlimited amounts of their wine in sealed containers, seven days a week. The victory of this law, as told by Jack Aellen of Linganore Winecellars, allowed wineries to fully participate in the tourism industry, to draw attention to the state wineries and to increase sales at winery tasting rooms. More challenges lay ahead, and the wineries knew that to be successful in the revision of Maryland's alcohol law, they would need professional assistance.

The Maryland Wineries Association hired the lobbying firm Rifkin, Livingston, Levitan and Silver in 1998.

In 2000, Maryland House Bill 414 passed, allowing state wineries to sell wine by the glass and to bring product onto retail-licensed premises for promotional activities. The Class 4 legislation also included the ability for wineries to apply for a Special Event Permit, of which they could use twelve a year, and only three per county until they reached their limit of twelve. These permits allow wineries to take their product off-site to sample and sell at non-licensed premises.

In 2003, "the Association of Maryland Wineries support[ed] SB514, a bill which facilitated the importation of wines not available within the State by Maryland wine consumers. By allowing out-of-state wineries to

The bill signing of HB414 in 2000. *Courtesy of Lucia Simmons, Linganore Winecellars at Berrywine Plantation.*

ship directly to a retail store of the buyer's choice, SB514 eases the process the buyer and the shipping winery must go through, which is a benefit to the consumer." But as the bill made its way through the legislature, it was altered with language that proposed the wholesaler and retailer lobby, which created a law that was unworkable and, ultimately, never used. It allowed only wines not distributed in Maryland to be delivered and required the wines to go through a Maryland wholesaler before being delivered to a retailer. Both the retailer and wholesaler had to opt-in and could charge a handing fee. In the years following the law's passage, no wholesaler ever agreed to participate in the law.

WINE AND GRAPE ADVISORY COMMITTEE

It started in a meeting in Hagerstown in September 2004. Senator Donald Munson was querying University of Maryland viticulturalist Dr. Joe Fiola about the prospects for a vibrant wine industry in Washington County, Maryland. Senator Munson had learned of grape growing in Washington County from Richard Penna, Maryland Grape Growers Association member and owner of Antietam Vineyard. Fiola replied to Senator Munson that the land was perfect for vineyards and the tourism base was already there—but no one was doing it.

Senator Munson wanted to know why and quickly called Maryland Department of Agriculture Secretary Lewis Riley. He asked Secretary Riley to form a task force to investigate the Maryland wine industry and learn how to promote its growth.

Secretary Riley quickly appointed the Maryland Wine and Grape Advisory Committee to identify strategies to facilitate the growth of Maryland's commercial vineyards and wineries and to offer recommendations to strengthen and expand Maryland's grape and wine economics and their markets. This report outlined a series of recommendations that, when implemented, would encourage and assist the continued expansion of Maryland's wine industry, as expressed by the growth in the number of vineyards, the acreage planted to wine grapes, the number of Maryland wineries, the gallons of wine produced in the state, the quality of that wine and the economic benefit to the state.

After several months of meetings, the committee issued a report called "Maryland Wine: The Next Vintage." This report was a full analysis of the state wine and grape industry and created a report listing of fifty-five recommendations to further industry growth. The report says, "The recommendations contained in this report seek to make Maryland a welcome and attractive state for investors to plant vineyards and open wineries. They seek to modernize liquor laws related to wine making and marketing that were enacted in the thirties following the repeal of prohibition."

When the report was released in December 2004, Maryland had only fifteen wineries, and the report noted the tremendous growth in neighboring states of Virginia and Pennsylvania and indicated that Maryland was behind in winery growth trends.

The fifty-five recommendations covered various topics. They were broken down into a number of categories, including the recognition of wine and grape growing as agriculture and the suggestion of land mapping programs, clean-vine projects, industry support from the University of Maryland, governmental and institutional support, legislative and regulatory changes to further industry growth, industry marketing, promotional research, education, tourism and economic development support, cooperative opportunities and wine and grape industry research.

There was compelling evidence that the Maryland wine industry lagged behind the rest of the nation—and most notably its northern and southern neighbors, Pennsylvania and Virginia—in both grape and wine production. Even when calculated on a per-capita or per-square-mile basis, Pennsylvania and Virginia out-produced Maryland in grapes and wine. The good news was that the Maryland wine industry was showing definite signs of growth. With the assistance of the state through investment in the industry, this growth could be not only sustained but also increased dramatically.

The experience of other states has shown that where states invest modestly in their wine industries, the return in the growth of that industry as measured in volume of wine grapes produced, gallons of wine produced, economic return to the states and tax income has been substantial.

The report truly charted the modern path for the industry. Richard Penna, the original chairperson and instigator of the commission, passed away in 2011. His leadership and wisdom were essential during this commission's existence, and he will be dearly missed by the industry. Since the report was released, almost forty wineries have opened. Vineyard acreage has tripled.

The most notable recommendation of the report was the creation of a formal Wine and Grape Advisory Commission in statute. In July 2005, the Governor's Advisory Commission on Maryland Wine and Grape Growing was formally created in statute. The commission was created to advise the Maryland Wine and Grape Promotion Council on the allocation of funds from the Maryland Wine and Grape Promotion Fund. The commission also was designed to identify strategies to facilitate the growth of viticulture in Maryland. Nine members constitute the commission. Seven of these are appointed to three-year terms by the governor. One member is named by the senate president and one by the house speaker.

The other notable product of the committee-driven legislation was the Maryland Wine and Grape Promotion Fund. This fund received moneys in 2005 and 2006 to be used for education, research and promotion projects. The commission established grant parameters and received proposals, recommending some for funding to the Wine and Grape Promotion Council.

In 2008, the commission issued "Impediments to Growth," a report citing specific regulations and state and local statutes that impede the growth of wineries and vineyards. The report helped form the wine industry's legislative efforts over the course of the next two years. The 2010 Maryland Winery Modernization Act was designed to solve many of the impediments noted in the report.

Each January, the commission is responsible for collecting data to assist the secretary of agriculture in determining the supply of Maryland grapes. If the supply of in state–grown grapes does not meet the needs of the commercial wineries, wineries are granted permission to source their grapes from outside Maryland.

THE WINERIES' BATTLE TO RETAIN SELF-DISTRIBUTION

In May 2005, the Supreme Court ruled that states were legally required to offer out-of-state wineries the same opportunities as their in-state wineries. In other words, a state couldn't give its in-state wineries an advantage over out-of-state wineries for interstate commerce but, rather, had to treat in- and out-of-state wineries equally.

Concurrently, a winery owner in Pennsylvania filed suit with the State of Maryland because his winery couldn't directly sell product to Maryland's retailers (wine shops) and restaurants. He cited the fact that Maryland allowed its Class 4 wineries to self-distribute but did not allow out-of-state wineries to do so.

The Maryland state comptroller, William Donald Schaefer, called industry members and their representatives into a meeting and offered three options to resolve this situation. The first option was to either suspend the current law or let the legislature work the issue out. The second option was to give out-of-state wineries the ability to distribute directly. The third option was to allow no winery to self-distribute. The industry responded with a request to let all wineries, in and out of state, distribute. Taking away the ability for Maryland wineries to distribute would have been shattering to the industry.

Despite the local wineries' request to allow out-of-state wineries to self-distribute, a week and a half later, wineries got a letter in the mail saying that the state was going to level down and wineries would lose their ability to self-distribute. This caused a major reaction from local wineries. They took action by drafting legislation and finding senators and delegates to commit as sponsors of this legislation. The wholesale and retail industry were staunchly opposed to opening the law to out-of-state wineries and formed a coalition against the wineries' effort to create a constitutional law that would allow them to self-distribute.

The wineries, in a David and Goliath–style battle, were confident that they could win this fight. Kevin Atticks, executive director of the Maryland Wineries Association and one of the leaders of this organized fight, said that in 2006, the Maryland wine industry, with significant assistance from its lobbying firm, Rifkin, Livingston, Levitan and Silver, fought its most aggressive battle in Annapolis to date. "Our side was made of our local wineries, lobbyists, a few key legislators like Senators Don Munson, Mac Middleton and Delegate Virginia Clagett among others. The liquor lobby and Comptroller Schaefer, fighting aggressively against us."

Atticks remembers spending more time in Annapolis during the 2006 legislative session than at any other time, even during the 2011 battle for wineries' ability to direct-ship wine to consumers. He recalls being joined by a different winery owner each day of the week to spend time lobbying, talking about the issues and making strides toward success.

To gain insight on the effects of constitutionality, the Maryland wineries worked with Michael Millemann, a constitutional law professor from the University of Maryland. Milleman wrote a constitutional analysis of the constitutionality of Senate Bill 812, the proposed legislation to amend current state law to make Maryland wineries' self-distribution constitutional.

A Full-Bodied History

It was at this time that the opposing liquor lobby hired former governor Marvin Mandel to further its cause against the wineries. Governor Mandel was legally and ethically prohibited from lobbying because he held a position on the University of Maryland Board of Regents. The *Baltimore Sun* investigated Mandel's involvement, and the resulting articles created a major backlash against the liquor lobby. The tide changed toward the wineries' interest.

Until 2006, Maryland's wineries were allowed to deliver their product to any store or restaurant that held a license. The legislation enacted in 2006 created a "Class 6 Limited Wine" wholesale license and a corresponding "non-resident winery" permit, which makes the local wineries' ability to self-distribute constitutional. Today, there are about three hundred out-of-state wineries that have the same ability as local wineries and can distribute directly to restaurants and wine shops. Part of drafting legislation to amend the old law required some negotiation between the wineries and the liquor lobby. Originally, wineries wanted the law to state that all wineries in the state of Maryland could self-distribute. Milleman quickly advised the association that if every winery in the state were covered, the law would still be unconstitutional. This meant that local wineries had to give something up—wineries over a certain size would have to be carried by a distributor. This posed a problem for some wineries that wanted to be carried by a distributer *and* self-distribute. Atticks remembers wild negotiations about the size of the wineries that would be legally required to be carried by a distributer. The number settled on was 27,500 gallons. Wineries that produced more than 27,500 gallons were required to have their product be carried by a distributer. Wineries that produced fewer than 27,5000 gallons could *either* be carried by a distributor *or* could self-distribute, but not both. It was a difficult negotiation within the association; the larger wineries in the state agreed that they would never be able to go back to the self-distribution system. To say this caused some angst with certain wineries would be an understatement, but the result benefited the industry as a whole.

The year 2006 was the Maryland wineries' first effort of truly going head to head with the liquor lobby and winning, hands down, and this was the first time in legislative history that the wineries, represented as an industry, were respected as an entity.

More Legislative Successes and the Winery Modernization Act

The Maryland Farm Bureau adopted a policy in 2007 that created a model definition of a winery. This definition stated the following:

> We support the recognition of vineyards and wineries—and their related activities—as agriculture. We support the definition of winery to include vineyards, processing of grapes, wine making, storage of wine, promotional events, tasting rooms, food service and other associated activities. We support the recognition of wineries as usage of right in agricultural and rural conservation zones.

In addition to "Maryland Wine: The Next Vintage," the Governor's Advisory Commission on Maryland Wine and Grape Growing created another report in 2008, titled "Impediments to Growth." In the fall of 2008, wineries and MWA began to meet with county commissioners and county liquor boards around the state to present the idea for what was called a Class W winery license concept, addressing the impediments listed in the commission's recent report. From these meetings, MWA garnered support for thirteen local bills in thirteen separate counties to support this Class W license, controlled by the liquor boards. Despite widespread support for these thirteen bills, all died in committee in 2009 due to strong opposition from the liquor lobby.

Through the support of the recently elected comptroller, Peter Franchot, legislative committee chairs and all alcohol industry representatives were brought together to urge them to assist local wineries in the passage of a statewide solution—one that would help wineries by reforming the winery laws while doing no harm to the other segments of the alcohol industry. This group met numerous times before presenting consensus language to the General Assembly in January 2010.

Lobbyist Pat Roddy and MWA executive director Kevin Atticks—with the guidance of the MWA Government Affairs Committee and many efforts by individual wineries—worked throughout the legislative session, meeting with legislators, regulators and county/regional delegations to achieve a major success in the passage of the Maryland Winery Modernization Act. The law passed with unanimous votes from each committee and from both the House of Delegates and the Senate.

The actual legislation addressed many issues. Before the legislation, sampling, sales of wine by the glass and open bottle—customary activities at regional wineries—were all limited or outright prohibited, depending on the jurisdiction. Before the Modernization Act, wineries were required to give tours to guests who were to sample wines. While some wineries give tours throughout the day, it was nearly impossible to offer every single guest a tour before doing a tasting. This issue was resolved. Legal hours of operation were not clear previously. The new law set legal hours from 10:00 a.m. to 10:00 p.m., with a caveat that guests visiting after 6:00 p.m. must be attending a special promotional event at the winery.

The new legislation also addressed food service and manufacturing and winemaking abilities of a winery. With the new legislation, wineries are able to manufacture, ferment and process wine and pomace brandy (spirits) at other Class 3 or 4 wineries. This solves many issues for start-up wineries that have yet to purchase major equipment. It also allows wineries to distill pomace brandy for use in ports, among other things.

In 2010, the grape and wine industry also formed a Political Action Committee, an additional step in bringing the industry into line with the rest of the alcohol industry.

OBTAINING THE RIGHT TO DIRECT-SHIP TO CONSUMERS

Wine shipping or direct-to-consumer shipping is the ability for a winery to sell wine and ship it directly to a customer's doorstep. Maryland's wineries had the ability to ship their wines to only customers whose state laws allowed them to receive wine by mail. While Maryland wineries could ship to many of their out-of-state customers, they were prohibited from shipping to their own in-state customers. This proved problematic when wineries couldn't form wine clubs or meet the needs of faraway customers. In 2011, thirty-seven states, plus the District of Columbia, allowed the shipping of wine to consumers by mail. After thirty years of effort, Maryland finally joined the ranks in that year.

The passing of direct shipping was a major lobbying undertaking that required the understanding and compromises of the entire alcohol industry and the cooperation of the key legislators in the appropriate committees. In 2010, Senate Bill 858 was passed. This law required state Comptroller Peter Franchot's office to create a study and report about the effects that direct shipping would have on state residents. The major concerns voiced by opposed parties were that the passing of direct-shipping legislation would allow underage residents to purchase wine, that it would have a negative affect on the wholesalers and distributers of wine and that it would be the first step in the demolition of the "three-tier system"—the system, set after the repeal of Prohibition, in which alcohol is distributed to Maryland residents.

This *Direct Wine Shipment Study* was submitted to the General Assembly on December 31, 2010, just in time for the 2011 legislative session. The study reviewed other states' direct-shipping regulations and the effect that they had on businesses and residents and found that the ability for residents to receive wine by mail would not shatter the three-tier system or put alcohol into the hands of minors.

The MWA worked cooperatively with many different organizations and interest groups, including the Wine Institute, an organization whose aim is to allow California wineries to ship to residents of all fifty states. The main consumer-driven organization that was helpful in passing this legislation was a consumer activist group called the Marylanders for Better Beer and Wine Laws, led by Adam Borden.

The combined effort of all invested parties, the report done by the comptroller's office and the voice of the consumer was a winning combination for the direct-shipping effort. After months of negotiations and compromises, the liquor lobby agreed to support the direct-shipping legislation. On May 10, 2011, Governor Martin O'Malley signed a bill that allows consumers in Maryland to receive wine shipments by mail from wineries with a direct-wine shipment permit issued by the comptroller of Maryland. Since Prohibition, that had been considered a felony. Maryland wineries can remember testifying in favor of direct-shipment law for the past thirty years. They were finally successful in their attempt.

The end of a vineyard row of Cabernet Franc at Fiore Winery and Distillery. *Courtesy of W. Michael Tirone Photography, michaeltirone.com.*

Cellar tool. *Courtesy of Danielle Grilli Marcus.*

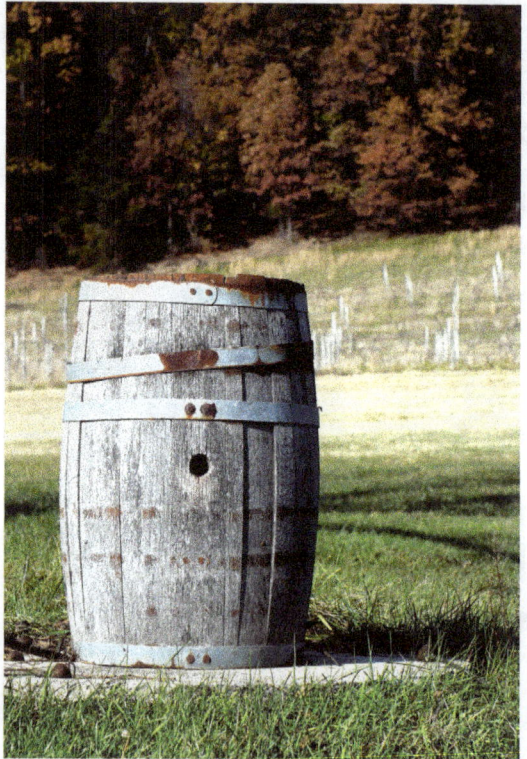

Lone barrel in a field at Woodhall Wine Cellars. *Courtesy of Danielle Grilli Marcus.*

Left: Ham Mowbray testing his wine. *Courtesy of Leslie A. Hubbard.*

Below: Pinot Grigio vine during bud break at Boordy Vineyards. *Courtesy of Rob Deford.*

The sorting belt at Boordy Vineyards. *Courtesy of Rob Deford.*

A shot of Black Ankle Vineyards submitted to the Maryland Wineries Association for its annual photo competition. *Courtesy of Susan Ledford.*

One lucky bunch. This is the photo competition winner from the 2011 annual photo competition. *Courtesy of W. Michael Tirone Photography, michaeltirone.com.*

The Boordy Vineyard Wine Glass

This is Philip Wagner's wine glass design. The glass was made to his specifications and was distributed by Boordy Vineyards. *Courtesy of Boordy Vineyards.*

Robert Deford Sr. and Anne Deford pruning grapevines with their grandson Phineas in arm. Phineas, son of Robert Deford Jr., is now involved in the family winery business. *Courtesy of Boordy Vineyards.*

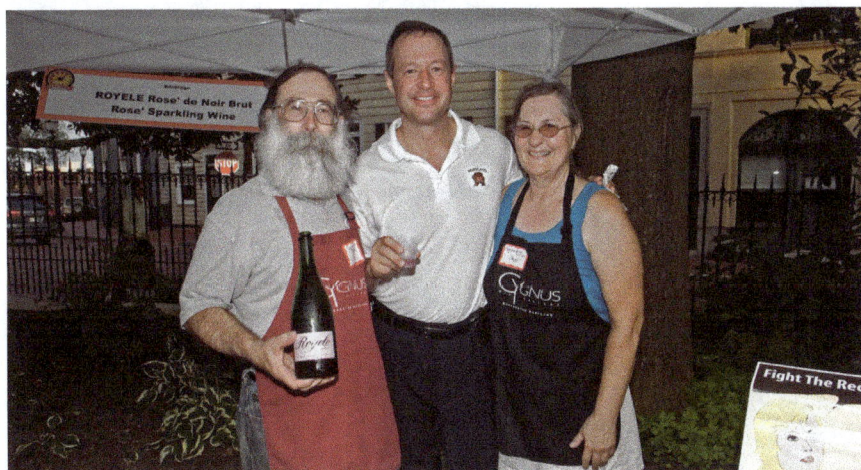

Ray Brasfield and Joyce Hongsermeier, owners of Cygnus Wine Cellars, with Governor Martin O'Malley at the Maryland Buy Local Picnic hosted at Government House in Annapolis each summer. Cygnus Wine Cellars was invited to offer samples of its sparkling wines. *Courtesy of Kevin Atticks.*

A wintertime photograph of the vineyard at Silver Run, home of Montbray Wine Cellars. *Courtesy of Leslie A. Hubbard.*

Lynne Rich, owner of Little Ashby Vineyards, on a tractor planting rows of grapes. Lynne passed away in 2011 and is dearly missed. *Courtesy of Warren Rich.*

Ray Brasfield behind the sampling station at one of the Maryland Wine Festivals. *Courtesy of Kevin Atticks.*

Bert Basignani on his tractor during harvest time. *Courtesy of Kevin Atticks.*

Left: The Wye Mills Vineyard, home of the oldest commercially grown vinifera grapes on the Eastern Shore. *Courtesy of St. Michaels Winery.*

Below: Paul Roberts at the entrance to Deep Creek Cellars. *Courtesy of Kevin Atticks.*

Above: Rose Fiore and Lynne Basignani at the launch of the Piedmont Wine Trail. *Courtesy of Kevin Atticks.*

Below: A map of the state wine trails as of 2011. *Courtesy of the Maryland Wineries Association.*

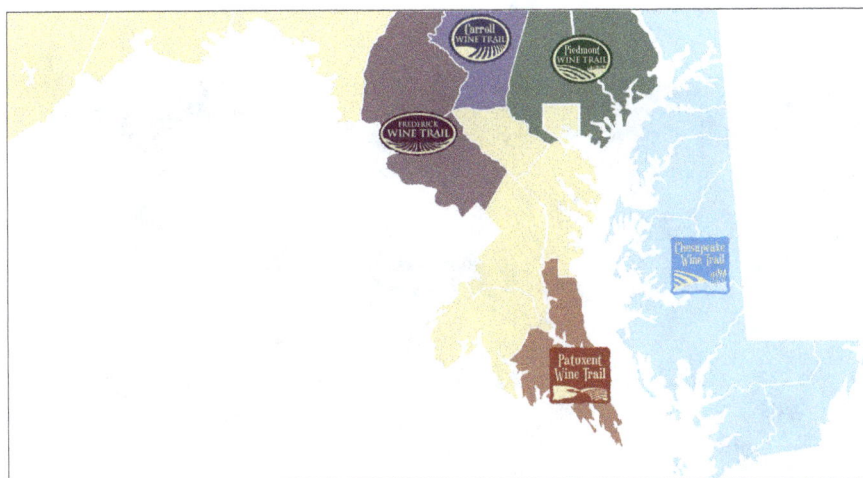

Above: Eric Aellen, Lucia Simmons, Lucille and Jack Aellen and Anthony and Mary Anne Aellen in front of their solar panel system, which provides solar energy for their electric car–charging station. *Courtesy of Lucia Simmons, Linganore Winecellars at Berrywine Plantation.*

Below: Hemsley Fortune, a vineyard operated by Wick Dudley on the Eastern Shore. *Courtesy of St. Michaels Winery.*

Above: The vineyard at Catoctin Breeze Vineyards. *Courtesy of Voytek Fiztya.*

Below: Governor Robert Ehrlich toasting a legislative victory at Boordy Vineyards with a number of Maryland winery owners, including Mike Fiore, Eric Aellen, Al Copp, Lynne Basignani, Ray Brasfield, Ed Boyce and Rob Deford. *Courtesy of Kevin Atticks.*

Above: Owner of Bordeleau Vineyards and Winery, Tom Shelton, showing his tidy vineyard with bird netting. *Courtesy of Kevin Atticks.*

Left: Vineyard watchdogs at Basignani Winery. *Courtesy of Kevin Atticks.*

Right: Planting vineyard rows. *Courtesy of Kevin Atticks.*

Below: Owners of Black Ankle Vineyards, Ed Boyce and Sarah O'Herron, walking through a vineyard. *Courtesy of Kevin Atticks.*

White wine grapes. *Courtesy of Duane Heaton.*

Chapter 8

The Future of the Industry

Wine as Agriculture

Vineyards are a sustainable crop option for Maryland farms. Grapes are a value-added crop, meaning that they can be produced into a product that is worth more than its original form, just as cheese is a value-added product compared to milk. Vineyards are not only low impact on the soils and farmland they inhabit, but they are also good for the beloved Chesapeake Bay.

Despite the fact that vineyards and grape growing are purely agricultural, it wasn't seen that way until recently. There were many leaders of the agricultural community who said grapes would never grow well in Maryland, while our neighboring states' vineyard industries flourished. At the turn of the century, members of the agricultural community began to recognize the potential for grapes to become a prize crop for Maryland farms.

Grape growers who have seen the many ebbs and flows from the early years of the industry indicate two major successes in grape growing over the last sixty years. The first success was finding and distributing an effective spray schedule for grape growers to follow. The second was recognition of ripeness and maturity in grapes. Lucie Morton and Paul Steiner were major influences in the leap in vineyard improvement.

While Maryland has always suffered and continues to suffer from a lack of locally grown grape availability, the growth in acreage and variety of grapes

The barrel room. *Courtesy of Sugarloaf Mountain Vineyard, photographer Richard Cress.*

grown over the history of the industry has been incredible. In 2010, the Maryland Grape Growers Association created a survey on grape production in Maryland. This survey was distributed to 240 grape growers, including wineries, some commercial grape growers and a small percentage of hobby grape growers. Results came back showing that in 2010, there were 150 vineyards, 601 acres of land under vine and 949 tons of grapes harvested. Since 2008, this industry has seen a 19 percent increase in number of vines and a 12 percent increase in number of acres.

Maryland boasts about ninety different varieties of grapes in the ground, and there is at least one vineyard in each county in the state. Most grapes are grown in Frederick County, followed by Carroll County. A close second is Queen Anne's County. Washington County shows potential to surge ahead as a leading county in grape acreage in the coming years.

Red vinifera grapes make up almost half of the grapes planted in Maryland, with Cabernet Sauvignon, Merlot and Cabernet Franc. The most plentiful white grapes are Chardonnay and Vidal Blanc.

In 2011, the majority of new vineyard plantings were Cabernet Franc, Chardonnay, Albariño, Syrah, Merlot and Petit Verdot. Gruner Veltliner, Melody and Sauvignon Blanc are three varieties that are becoming much more popular for the state grape growers as well.

These numbers show that there has been more than a 200 percent increase in vineyard acreage from 2001 to 2010. Part of the surge in number of commercial vineyards and their acreage is due to commercial vineyard management companies. There are currently three of these companies in the state, the oldest being Schmidt Vineyard Management. Jennie Schmidt of Schmidt Vineyard Management is also the current president of the Maryland Grape Growers Association. She manages vineyards on the Eastern Shore, and her family has their own commercial vineyard as well.

TOBACCO FARMS INTO VINEYARDS

In 2000, the Tri-County Council of Southern Maryland issued a grant to the Maryland Department of Agriculture and the Maryland Cooperative Extension to create a program to teach tobacco farmers about other types of crops to grow—including grapes—as tobacco became a less-than-desirable crop. The goals of this grant were not necessarily to start new wineries but were more focused on tobacco growers having another value-added crop that they could sell to current commercial wineries.

The result can be seen while driving through the Patuxent Wine Trail. Where tobacco fields used to be there are now vineyards spotted with old tobacco barns along historic routes.

GROWING REGIONS AND AMERICAN VITICULTURAL AREAS

The state of Maryland—often called America in Miniature because of its vast landscapes and varying terrain—is broken up into four separate grape-growing regions. These naturally bound regions have lent themselves to become distinct winery locations.

The Piedmont Plateau is the region in central Maryland in which most of the state's vineyards are planted. The Piedmont Plateau stretches from the foothills west of Frederick to the top of the Chesapeake Bay. This area contains wineries in Frederick, Baltimore and Harford Counties.

The Eastern Shore is the region that extends from the upper shore down to the lower shore, containing Cecil, Kent, Queen Anne's, Talbot, Dorchester, Caroline, Somerset, Worcester and Wicomico Counties. This region is growing extremely fast in number of wineries and vineyards. It is known for its warm days and cool evenings, sandy and well-drained soil and moderate climate.

Maryland's third growing region, the Southern Plain, is home to the Patuxent Wine Trail. It includes Anne Arundel, Prince George's, Calvert, Charles and St. Mary's Counties. The temperatures are warmer in the Southern Plain, which lends itself to become a great spot for southern Italian and other Mediterranean grape varieties.

The fourth growing region, the Western Mountains, covers Washington, Allegany and Garrett Counties. New grape growers and winemakers are taking big strides in these regions, planting upward of twenty acres of grapes at a time. Because of its cooler climate, cold-hearty grapes thrive here.

The first American Viticultural Area, or AVA, formed was the Linganore AVA. Jack Aellen of Linganore Winecellars prepared the argument for this AVA in 1983. The Cumberland AVA was formed in 1985, quickly followed by the Catoctin AVA, which was pushed forward by Bret Byrd and Bob Lyon in 1987.

MODERN CONNECTIONS

In 2010, the Maryland Wineries Association launched a brand-new website. Included in the site is a database of all wines available in the state of Maryland. A company called Mission Media out of Baltimore created the site. One of the most inventive parts of the site is the ability for wineries to log on to update and edit their contact and product information.

The local wine industry has also become very active with social media in recent years, especially with Facebook and Twitter. These are new avenues for wineries to get in touch with their customer base and to create new customers.

The local blogging community has also taken note, and blogs are developing for the specific intent of covering local wine news. Maryland wineries take part in conferences along the East Coast like the Drink Local Wine Conference.

THE FUTURE OF THE MARYLAND WINE INDUSTRY

The survey completed by the Maryland Grape Growers Association in 2010 predicts that by the end of 2015, Maryland will be home to over seventy-five wineries and at least nineteen more commercial grape growers.

A vibrant wine industry is made of more than just a high-quality product. A healthy industry requires a high-quality grape-growing environment, skilled winemakers, a receptive and open market, laws and regulations that support the industry rather than hinder it and a common place for industry members to gather, share, learn and grow from one another.

With the passing of consistently positive legislation (including the ability for wineries to self-distribute their products), winery modernization legislation and the ability for wineries to ship wine to consumers' homes, the state legislation has become more winery-friendly and the public has more access to local wine.

Most states with active wine industries have at least one state association or collaborative effort to support their wineries. These groups are either branches of the local department of agriculture or separate entities dependent on state funding. One of the Maryland wine industry's biggest assets is an active and involved state trade association, the Maryland Wineries Association. This nonprofit trade association is completely independent of

Bud break. *Courtesy of Voytek Fizyta.*

state funding. The MWA provides resources for wineries in all aspects of their businesses. It is made up of several committees, including legislative; festivals and events; marketing; education; and more. These committees take the pulse of the industry to see what areas are lacking or need more support or help in development or programs. From there, the committees make recommendations to the board, which is made up of a representative from each winery. The MWA is completely self-funded and depends not on expensive yearly member dues but, rather, creates its own revenue stream through festivals and events, which also expand the message and promotion of the local wine industry.

Each winery that opens in each county of Maryland widens the pathway and eases the journey for future wineries. Each winery that tries a new method or plants a new variety of grape leads the whole group a step further. Each of these efforts, whether in business, marketing, viticulture or winemaking, creates a positive tide that lifts all boats.

It is safe to say that the progress that the Maryland wine industry is making will continue to move along steadily. More wineries will open. Old wineries will usher in new wineries, sharing secrets, equipment and a slice of the market. New wineries will challenge old wineries to improve vintage after vintage. They will invest in new equipment and new consultants, and the rest of the industry will need to keep up. In the words of Lucie Morton:

> *Maryland now appears to recognize economic advantages to supporting wine growing in the state. There are family farms, historic houses and other farmland where vineyards are having and will have a positive impact on the local scene. Out of these vineyards, now growing beyond the pioneering stage, there will be a need for wineries and hospitality venues. Out of these vineyards already are coming wines that reflect professionalism and a potential for distinction that was just beginning a few decades ago.*

A Listing of Maryland Wineries

Aliceanna Winery
Baltimore, MD
724-699-1335
aliceannawinery.com

Basignani Winery (Piedmont Wine Trail)
15722 Falls Road
Sparks, MD 21152
410-472-0703
basignani.com

Berrywine Plantations/Linganore Winecellars (Frederick Wine Trail)
13601 Glissans Mill Road
Mount Airy, MD 21771-8599
410-795-6432
linganorewines.com

Black Ankle Vineyards (Frederick Wine Trail)
14463 Black Ankle Road
Mount Airy, MD 21771
301-829-3338
blackankle.com

Boordy Vineyards (Piedmont Wine Trail)
12820 Long Green Pike
Hydes, MD 21082
410-592-5015
boordy.com

Bordeleau Vineyards and Winery (Chesapeake Wine Trail)
3155 Noble Farm Road
Eden, MD 21822
410-677-3334
bordeleauwine.com

Cascia Vineyards—Opening Soon! (Chesapeake Wine Trail)
1200 Thompson Creek Road
Stevensville, MD 21666
410-604-2127

Cassinelli Vineyards and Winery (Chesapeake Wine Trail)
3830 Church Hill Road
Church Hill, MD 21623
410-925-6181
cassinelliwinery.com

Catoctin Breeze Vineyard (Frederick Wine Trail)
15184 Roddy Road
Thurmont, MD 21788
240-449-0677
catoctinbreeze.com

Costa Ventosa Winery and Vineyard (Chesapeake Wine Trail)
9031 Whaleyville Road
Whaleyville, MD 21872
410-352-9867
costaventosa.com

Cove Point Winery (Patuxent Wine Trail)
755 Cove Point Road
Lusby, MD 20657
410-326-0949
covepointwinery.com

Cygnus Wine Cellars (Carroll Wine Trail)
3130 Long Lane
Manchester, MD 21102
410-374-6395
cygnuswinecellars.com

A Listing of Maryland Wineries

Deep Creek Cellars
177 Frazee Ridge Road
Friendsville, MD 21531
301-746-4349
deepcreekcellars.com

DeJon Vineyards (Piedmont Wine Trail)
5300 Hydes Road
Hydes, MD 21082
443-253-9802
dejonvineyard.com

Detour Vineyard and Winery (Carroll Wine Trail)
7933 Forest and Stream Club Road
Detour, MD 21757-8751
410-775-0220
detourwinery.com

Distillery Lane Ciderworks (Frederick Wine Trail)
5533 Gapland Road
Jefferson, MD 21755
301-834-8920
ciderapples.com

Dove Valley Winery (Chesapeake Wine Trail)
645 Harrington Road
Rising Sun, MD 21911
410-658-8388
dovevalleywine.com

Elk Run Vineyards (Frederick Wine Trail)
15113 Liberty Road
Mount Airy, MD 21771
410-775-2513
elkrun.com

Far Eastern Shore Winery—Opening Soon! (Chesapeake Wine Trail)
Easton, MD
410-829-5305
fareasternshorewinery.com

Fiore Winery (Piedmont Wine Trail)
3026 Whiteford Road
Pylesville, MD 21132
410-879-4007
FioreWinery.com

Frederick Cellars (Frederick Wine Trail)
Everedy Square/Shab Row
221 North East Street
Frederick, MD 21701
301-668-0311
frederickcellars.com

Fridays Creek Winery (Patuxent Wine Trail)
3485 Chaneyville Road
Owings, MD 20736
410-286-WINE
fridayscreek.com

Galloping Goose Vineyard (Carroll Wine Trail)
4326 Maple Grove Road
Hampstead, MD 21074
410-374-6596
gallopinggoosevineyards.com

Great Shoals Winery
26431 Mason Webster Road
Princess Anne, MD 21853
410-849-9616
greatshoals.com

Harford Vineyard (Piedmont Wine Trail)
1311 West Jarrettsville Road
Forest Hill, MD 21050
443-495-1699
harfordvineyard.com

Knob Hall Winery
14108 St. Paul Road
Clear Spring, MD 21722
301-842-2777
knobhallwinery.com

Layton's Chance Vineyard and Winery (Chesapeake Wine Trail)
4225 New Bridge Road
Vienna, MD 21869
410-228-1205
laytonschance.com

Legends Vineyard (Piedmont Wine Trail)
521 Asbury Road
Churchville, MD 21028
410-914-5122
legendsvineyardmd.com

Little Ashby Vineyards (Chesapeake Wine Trail)
27549 Ashby Drive
Easton, MD 21601
410-819-8850
littleashbyvineyards.com

Loew Vineyards (Frederick Wine Trail)
14001 Liberty Road
Mount Airy, MD 21771
301-831-5464
loewvineyards.com

Mount Felix Vineyard and Winery (Piedmont Wine Trail)
2000 Level Road
Havre de Grace, MD 21078
410-939-0913
mountfelix.com

Orchid Cellar Winery (Frederick Wine Trail)
8546 Pete Wiles Road
Middletown, MD 21769
301-473 3568
orchidcellar.com

Penn Oaks Winery
11 Midhurst Road
Silver Spring, MD 20910
301-562-8592

Perigeaux Vineyards and Winery (Patuxent Wine Trail)
8650 Mackall Road
St. Leonard, MD 20685
410-586-2710
perigeaux.com

Port of Leonardtown Winery (Patuxent Wine Trail)
23190 Newtowne Neck Road
Leonardtown, MD 20650
301-690-2192
portofleonardtown.com

Romano Vineyard and Winery
15715 Bald Eagle School Road
Brandywine, MD 20613
301-752-1103
romanowinery.com

Royal Rabbit Vineyards
1090 Jordan Sawmill Road
Parkton, MD 21120
443-721-6692
royalrabbitvineyards.com

Running Hare Vineyard (Patuxent Wine Trail)
150 Adelina Road
Prince Frederick, MD 20678
410-414-8486
runningharevineyard.com

Serpent Ridge Vineyard (Carroll Wine Trail)
2962 Nicodemus Road
Westminster, MD 21157
410-848-6511
serpentridge.com

Slack Winery (Patuxent Wine Trail)
16040 Woodlawn Lane
Ridge, MD 20650
301-872-5175
slackwine.com

Solomons Island Winery (Patuxent Wine Trail)
515 Garner Lane
Lusby, MD 20657
410-394-1933
solomonsislandwinery.com

St. Michaels Winery (Chesapeake Wine Trail)
605 South Talbot Street #6
St. Michaels, MD 21663
410-745-0808
st-michaels-winery.com

Sugarloaf Mountain Vineyard (Frederick Wine Trail)
18125 Comus Road
Dickerson, MD 20842
301-605-0130
smvwinery.com

Terrapin Station Winery (Chesapeake Wine Trail)
80 Ricketts Mill Road
Elkton, MD
410-398-1875
terrapinstationwinery.com

Thanksgiving Farm
Harwood, MD 20776
410-630-1151
thanksgivingfarm.com

Tilmon's Island Winery
755 Millington Road
Sudlersville, MD 21668
443-480-5021
tilmonswine.com

Woodhall Wine Cellars
17912 York Road
Parkton, MD 21120
410-357-8644
woodhallwinecellars.com

Glossary

ACIDITY: Grapes contain several acids, but the main ones are tartaric and malic. A little acidity in wine gives it a "fresh" taste, but too much will make the wine "tart" or "sour."

AFTERTASTE: The taste that remains in the mouth just after swallowing a sip of wine.

AGING: The storing of wine. Aging of wines in bottles, in some instances, improves taste and aroma. Long periods of aging red wines in oak barrels can add to its complexity.

AIR LOCK: A device that allows fermentation gasses to pass out of the fermenter while preventing outside air from entering.

ALCOHOL: Ethyl alcohol, or ethanol, is the only type of alcohol present in wine (in significant amounts). If a wine contains too much alcohol, it may impart a "hot" taste, whereas too little may leave a wine lacking in body or unbalanced.

AMERICAN VITICULTURAL AREA (AVA): A geographic area designated by the Bureau of Alcohol, Tobacco and Firearms and characterized by that area's topography, soil, microclimate and historical precedent.

AMPELOGRAPHY (am-peh-LAW-gra-fee): A book that describes the structural characteristics of various varieties of grapevines.

AMPHORA (AM-fuhr-uh): An ancient vessel used to store and transport wine.

ANTHER: The male (pollen-producing) part of the grape flower.

APERITIF (ah-pehr-uh-TEEF): Any wine served before a meal. Traditionally, aperitifs were vermouths and other similar wines flavored with herbs and spices.

APPEARANCE: A term used to describe whether a wine is crystal clear (brilliant), cloudy or contains sediment.

APPELLATION (ap-puh-LAY-shuhn): A term used to define the vineyard location where the grapes were grown for a specific wine. A wine whose label states "Napa County" (the appellation) must have been made at least 85 percent from grapes that were grown in Napa County.

ARGOLS: The name given to raw cream of tartar crystals found in chunks adhering to the sides and bottoms of wine tanks.

AROMA: The smell or fragrance from wine that has its origin in the grape, as opposed to "bouquet," which has its origin in the processing or aging methods.

ASSEMBLAGE (ah-sahm-BLAHJ): The blending together of component wine lots to form a final composite intended for bottling, aging, sparkling wine production or some other use by the winemaker.

ASTRINGENCY: Sensation of taste, caused by tannins in wine, that is best described as mouth-drying, bitter or puckery.

ATMOSPHERE: Unit of measure for pressure inside a bottle of sparking wine or champagne. One atmosphere equals 14.7 pounds per square inch, and this is the standard atmospheric pressure at sea level in the world. Commercial sparkling wines commonly contain four to six atmospheres of CO_2 pressure at room temperature.

GLOSSARY

AURORE: A hybrid grape variety produced in the nineteenth century by French nurseryman Albert Seibel and still used, especially in the eastern United States, for sparkling wine production. Sometimes spelled aurora.

AUSLESE (OWS-lay-zuh): A German word meaning "selection." In German wine law, it means the wine is made only from specially selected, perfectly ripened bunches of grapes that are handpicked.

AUTOLYSIS (aw-TAHL-uh-sihss): The decomposition of dead yeast cells that occurs in wines that are aged "sur lie" (on the lees).

BACCHUS: 1. Roman god of wine. Not to be confused with Dionysus, who was the Greek god of wine before the age of Rome. 2. A German white wine grape.

BALANCE: 1. A subjective term used in wine evaluation. Wine in which the tastes of acid, sugar, tannin, alcohol and flavor are in harmony is said to be in balance. 2. In the vineyard, it's the relationship between grape clusters and shoot growth and is controlled by proper pruning practices.

BALLING: The name of a density scale for measuring sugar content in water base solutions. Grape juice is primarily sugar and water, and the balling scale is used for a quick and easy "sugar analysis" of juice. Balling and Brix often are used interchangeably. Each degree balling is equivalent to 1 percent of sugar in the juice. For example, grape juice that measures twenty-one degrees on the balling or Brix scale contains about 21 percent sugar.

BARREL FERMENTING: The act of fermenting grape juice in wooden barrels, as opposed to neutral containers (stainless steel, glass, plastic).

BARRELING DOWN: The act of placing wine into barrels for aging.

BATF: Bureau of Alcohol, Tobacco and Firearms, the U.S. federal agency that collects alcohol taxes and administers wine regulations.

BAUME (boh-MAY): A system for measuring the sugar content of grape juice by its density. Each degree Baume is equal to approximately 1.75 percent sugar in the juice.

BEAD: Colloquial term referring to the bubbles that float on top of a fermenting wine or champagne in the glass.

BEERENAUSLESE (BAY-ruhn-OWS-lay-zuh): Literally, "berry selection" in German. Beerenauslese wines are made from grapes that are picked individually rather than a whole bunch at a time. All grapes on a cluster or bunch do not normally ripen at exactly the same rate. Berry selection allows the winemaker to make superb wine by ensuring that every grape berry is at optimum ripeness.

BENTONITE: A natural clay that is used in fining (clearing) wines.

BERRY: A common name given to an individual grape.

BERRY SET: The fixing of tiny, newly pollinated berries to the stem.

BIANCO (BYAHN-koh): The Italian word for "white."

BIG: A subjective tasting term that refers to a rich, full-bodied wine.

BITTER: A subjective tasting term. Bitterness usually refers to tannin in wine and is sensed by taste buds along the sides of the tongue in the extreme rear.

BLACK ROT: A fungus disease of grapevines.

BLANC DE BLANC: A term referring to white wine made from white grapes.

BLANC DE NOIR: A term referring to white wine made from red grapes.

BLENDING: Combining two or more wines for the purpose of adjusting the flavor, aroma and other components to create a more desirable wine.

BLOOM: 1. The grape flower or blossom. Also the time of grape flowering. 2. The grayish, powdery film that occurs on grapes in the field and contains wild yeast and dust.

BODY: A tasting term referring to viscosity, thickness, consistency or texture. A wine with body often has higher alcohol or sugar content than others.

BORDEAUX (bohr-DOH): An area in southwest France considered by many to be one of the greatest wine-producing regions.

BORDEAUX MIXTURE: A mix of copper sulfate, lime and water used as a spray on grapevines to fight fungus diseases.

BOTRYTIS (boh-TRI-tihs): A fungus that grows on certain grapes as they ripen under certain weather conditions. Called "noble rot" because it concentrates both sugar and flavor.

BOUQUET: The smell or fragrance in wine, which has its origins in the wine production or aging methods.

BRANDY: The liquor obtained from distillation of wine and aged in wood.

BREATHING: Letting a bottle of wine stand for several minutes to several hours after pulling the cork but before serving it.

BRILLIANT: A sensory evaluation term to describe a wine which is crystal clear and absolutely free from sediment or cloudiness.

BRIX (BRIHKS): The unit of measurement of soluble solids (sugar) in ripening grapes. A reading of one degree Brix equals 1 percent sugar in the juice.

BRUT: A French term referring to the driest (least sweet) champagne. Drier than "extra dry."

BUD: A small swelling on a shoot or cane from which a new shoot develops.

BUD BREAK: The action of buds swelling and beginning new growth in spring.

BUNG: The hole in a barrel (or tank).

BURGUNDY: Located in eastern France, it's one of the most famous wine-growing areas.

BUTT: A "large" wine barrel, usually just over one hundred gallons in capacity. "Normal" barrel sizes are approximately fifty or sixty gallons in capacity.

CABERNET FRANC (KA-behr-nay FRAHNGK): A v. vinfera species of grape.

CABERNET SAUVIGNON (KA-behr-nay soh-vihn-YOHN): A v. vinfera species of grape.

CALYPTRA: The covering of an emerging grape flower.

CAMBIUM: The layer of living tissue under the bark and phloem tissue of a grapevine. New wood cells (xylem) form at the inside of cambium as it grows; new phloem and bark cells form at the outside edge. The net effect is to increase the diameter of the vine.

CANE: The mature shoot of a vine.

CANOPY: The leaves and shoots formed by a grapevine.

CAP: A tiny green cover that loosens and then falls off, exposing the pinhead-size ovary and releasing the pollinating anthers of an individual grape flower. When the cap falls off, the flower is said to be in bloom.

CAP STEM: The small length of stem that connects each individual grape berry to its bunch.

CAPSULE: The wrapping that covers the neck and cork of a wine bottle.

CARBON DIOXIDE (CO_2): A gas that occurs naturally in air. Vine leaves produce sugar from CO_2, sunlight and water. This sugar is the source of energy used by the vine for growth and grape production.

CARBONIC MACERATION: A process where wine grapes are not crushed but fermented whole. The process is used to make wines that are particularly light and fruity. This is the process commonly used to produce "nouveau" wines of the Beaujolais region of France.

CARBOY: A glass bottle used (usually by home vintners) to ferment and wine. They range in size from five to seven gallons.

CASK: Any wooden container used for wine aging or storage. The term includes barrels, butts, pipes, etc.

CEPAGE (say-PAHZH): French for grape variety.

CHABLIS: Wine region in central France named for the village near its center.

CHAMPAGNE: Sparkling wine produced in the Champagne region of France. Most U.S. wine producers use the term "sparkling wine" and may indicate that it was made by the French "méthode champenoise."

CHAPTALIZATION: The act of adding sugar to grape juice or must early in the fermentation to correct for natural deficiencies.

CHARACTER: A wine-tasting term referring to the style of taste.

CHARMAT PROCESS: A process developed by Eugene Charmat for producing sparkling wine or champagne cheaply and in large quantities by conducting the secondary fermentation in large tanks rather than individual bottles.

CHIANTI (kee-AHN-tee): Medium- to full-bodied red table wine of Tuscany in Italy. Chiantis are blends, but the primary grape variety used is sangiovese.

CHLOROPLASTS: Oval, chlorophyll-bearing structures inside the cells of leaves that act as factories to produce sugar for plant growth from CO_2 and water. The energy used for this conversion is sunlight, captured by the chlorophyll.

CLARET: Common name for the red wines of Bordeaux.

CLARITY: In wine evaluation, a subjective term for the absence of cloudiness or sediment in a wine.

CLONE: Grapevines descended from the same individual vine. One vine, found to have especially desirable characteristics, may be propagated by grafting or budding to produce a whole vineyard that is identical to the original vine.

CLOS: In France, a walled or enclosed vineyard. The word is now used in other countries as part of a name for a winery or wine label.

CLOSED-TOP TANKS: Fermentation tanks with permanent tops. These always have doors or vents in the top to facilitate cleaning and for monitoring fermentations.

CLOYING: A tasting term meaning the wine is difficult to enjoy because of excessive sweetness that stays in your mouth after the wine is gone.

CLUSTER: A bunch of grapes.

CLUSTER THINNING: The process of removing young grape clusters to control the size of the crop.

COARSE: A wine tasting term referring to an unfinished, rough or crude wine that is difficult to drink.

COLD STABILIZATION: The process of chilling wine to below thirty degrees Fahrenheit to precipitate potassium crystals out of solution.

COLD STABLE: A wine that can be kept in a refrigerator without forming a sediment or crystals is said to be cold stable.

COMPOUND BUD: The normal type of bud that appears at each node along a vine shoot or cane. It contains not one but three separate, partially developed shoots with rudimentary leaves in greatly condensed form. Usually, only the middle one grows when the bud pushes out in the spring. The others break dormancy only if the primary shoot is damaged.

COOPERAGE: A common term in general use to describe any container used for aging and storing wine. Cooperage includes barrels and tanks of all sizes.

CORDON: A French word (roughly translated means "arm") that refers to the permanent wood of a (usually horizontal) grapevine from which the fruiting wood is grown.

CORK: A cylinder-shaped piece cut from the thick bark of a cork-oak tree and used as a stopper in wine bottles. Cork is especially well suited for this purpose because of its waxy composition and springiness.

corky: A corky wine has an unpleasant odor and flavor of moldy cork.

corolla: An individual grape flower before it blossoms.

cream of tartar: A natural component of grape juice and wine. The chemical name is potassium bi-tartrate. Removed from wine as a byproduct, cream of tartar is used in cooking.

Cremant: A category of champagne that contains less carbonation than standard champagnes. Cremant champagnes are usually light and fruity.

crisp: A tasting term to describe good acidity and pleasant taste without excessive sweetness.

cru: French word for growth. It refers to a vineyard of especially high quality, such as a classified growth or "cru classe."

crush: The process of crushing and destemming wine grapes just prior to fermentation. "The crush" refers to the autumn season when grapes ripen and are fermented.

crush tank: The wine tank that receives the newly crushed must—pumped directly from the crusher.

crust: The sediment, often crystalline, that forms inside wine bottles during long bottle aging. It is often brittle and can break into pieces as the wine is being poured.

cultivar: A cultivated variety of grape.

cuvaison (koo-veh-ZOHN): The period of time when grape juice is kept in contact with the skins and seeds during fermentation.

cuvee (koo-VAY): A batch of wine usually held in a single tank or large cask. Cuvee often refers to a specific blend of still wines that was blended purposely for later champagne making.

decant: Pouring wine carefully from a bottle in which loose sediment would otherwise become stirred up. After decanting (carefully pouring off the clear wine until only the sediment remains behind), the sediment can be washed out of the bottle. Then the decanted wine can be returned to the clean bottle for serving.

DEGORGEMENT (disgorging): The act of removing the frozen plug of ice (containing spent yeast) from a champagne bottle after the riddling. Degorgement takes place on the bottling line just prior to adding dosage and the final corking of the finished bottle of champagne. See dosage.

DEMI-SEC: A champagne term signifying that the product is medium-sweet.

DESSERT WINE: Any of a class of sweet wines, usually fortified to higher alcohol content, which are served with desserts or as after-dinner drinks. Common dessert wines are ports, sherries, muscatel, Madeira, tokay and angelica.

DIONYSUS: Greek god of wine and revelry. See Bacchus.

DOSAGE: The few ounces of wine, often sweetened, which is added to each bottle of champagne after disgorging to make up for the liquid volume lost by disgorging.

DOWNY MILDEW: A fungal disease of grapevines that kills the affected tissue. The disease is native to eastern North America and has spread to Europe and most other regions of the world.

DRY: The complete absence of sugar in the wine.

EARLY HARVEST: These wines are produced in the coolest years when grape ripeness doesn't achieve full maturity. The wines are low in alcohol, light and easy to drink despite having high natural acidity. The German equivalent is trocken or halbtroken.

EARTHY: A sensory evaluation term for wine with a taste or smell reminiscent of soil, mushrooms or mustiness.

ENOLOGY: The science and technical study of winemaking.

GLOSSARY

ESTATE BOTTLED: A label phrase (implying quality) meaning that the wine was produced and bottled at the winery from grapes owned (and farmed) by the winery owners.

ESTERS: Aromatic flavor compounds that give fruits, juices and wines much of their "fruitiness."

ETHANOL (ETHYL ALCOHOL): The type of alcohol produced by yeast fermentation of sugar under ordinary conditions. The alcohol in alcoholic beverages is always ethanol.

FERMENTATION: The process carried out by yeast growth in grape juice (or other sugar solutions) by which sugar is transformed into ethyl alcohol and CO_2.

FERMENTED "ON THE SKINS": A statement made about a wine (almost always red) that was fermented with the juice and solids together. The solids are discarded after the fermentation is completed.

FERMENTERS: Tanks, barrels or other containers when used for fermentations.

FINING: The process of adding a material to wine in order to clarify it.

FINISH: The last impression left in the mouth by the taste of a wine.

FINISHING: The last steps in processing a wine before bottling, which may include bottling. Often, this includes fining, blending and filtration or centrifugation.

FINO: A term found on some sherry labels to denote the winery's lightest and driest sherries.

FLABBY: A tasting term for a wine that is too low in acidity, too high in pH and difficult to drink.

FLAT: A tasting term. Similar to flabby, a flat wine is lacking in acidity and crispness. Flat wines are difficult to drink and enjoy even if the flavor is good. In sparkling wines, flat means the wine lacks carbonation.

FLINTY: A tasting term used to describe wine with a hard, dry, clean taste reminiscent of flint struck by steel.

FLOWERY: A tasting term for wine with an exceptionally aromatic character reminiscent of fresh garden flowers.

FOXINESS: A tasting term to describe the smell and taste of Concord grapes and wine and the smell and taste of similar varieties of vitis labrusca.

FREE RUN JUICE: The juice that separates from must by draining alone (without pressing).

FRENCH/AMERICAN HYBRIDS: Grape varieties that did not occur in nature but were produced by crossbreeding (usually crosses between one or more native American varieties and one or more European traditional wine varieties).

FRUITFUL BUD: A bud that will grow into a fruit-bearing shoot.

FRUITY: A tasting term for wine that has retained the fresh flavor of the grapes used in its fermentation.

FUME BLANC: A name that has come to be synonymous with Sauvignon Blanc table wine.

GASSY: A sensory evaluation term describing a wine that contains residual carbon dioxide left over from the fermentation.

GENERIC WINE: Blended wine of ordinary quality, without any varietal or other special characteristics. Everyday, low-price wine.

GREEN: A tasting term describing the grassy, herbaceous or vegetal taste of wines that were grown in too cool a climate.

HEARTWOOD: The innermost portion of the woody tissue (xylem) making up the trunk of woody plants, such as grapevines or trees. Heartwood is composed of dead xylem cells, which serve to give wood its strength.

HEAT SUMMATION: A measure of the climate of a growing region calculated by adding the mean temperatures for each day (minus a base temperature) over a growing season. For grapes, the base temperature is fifty degrees Fahrenheit (ten degrees Celsius).

HERBACEOUSNESS: Refers to a vegetative taste in wine.

HOCK: A term used to describe the unusually tall bottle that is used for Riesling and similar wines. Also, hock refers to Riesling and similar wines themselves.

HOT: A taste sensation often found in high-alcohol wines.

HYBRID: In viticulture, a new variety resulting from crossing two other (often very different) varieties.

HYDROMETER: An instrument used to measure the specific gravity of a liquid.

ICE WINE: Wine made from frozen grapes. Ice wines are always sweet, usually light and also delicate.

INTERNODE: The section of a grapevine stem between two successive nodes or joints on the shoot or cane.

JEROBOAM: An oversize wine bottle; however, the exact size is not standardized. It may be equivalent to four, five or six standard (750-millileter) bottles, depending on the wine producer. In Champagne, France, and in California, it is often 3 liters in size; in Bordeaux, 3.75 liters; in England, as much as 4.5 liters.

JUG WINES: Common name given to wines sold at modest prices in 1.5-liter size or larger containers.

KEG: A small barrel for wine aging or storage—usually twelve to fifteen gallons in size.

LABRUSCA: A principal species of native North American grapes. Concord is the purest example currently grown on a large scale in the eastern United States.

LACTIC ACID: A natural organic acid that occurs in many foods. In wine, it exists only in trace amounts unless the wine has undergone a secondary malolactic fermentation.

LAMBRUSCO: Not to be confused with Labrusca. Produced in northern Italy, Lambruscos are sparkling red wines, usually sweet, light, fruity and pleasant to drink.

LATE HARVEST: Name given to dessert or full-bodied table wines produced from overripe grapes.

LEAF AXIL: The acute angle between a vine shoot and a leaf stem or petiole extending from the shoot. Buds develop in these axils just above each leaf petiole.

LEES: The sediment that settles to the bottom of the wine in a tank during processing. If primarily yeast, as from a fermentation, it is called "yeast lees"; if sediment from fining, it is called "fining lees."

LEGS: A term referring to the colorless droplets that form along the inside wall of a wine glass, just above the surface of the wine.

MACERATION: The act of soaking grape solids in their juice for certain time periods prior to fermentation of the juice.

MADERIZATION: Oxidation of table wines due to improper storage. Maderization gives Madeira wines part of their desirable character, but the same character is undesirable in normal table wines.

MAGNUM: An oversize bottle, twice the size of a standard 750-millileter wine bottle.

MALBEC: One of the major red wine grape varieties of Bordeaux.

MALIC ACID: A natural organic acid that occurs in ripe grapes in relatively high concentrations. It is the second most abundant organic acid in most varieties.

Glossary

MALOLACTIC FERMENTATION: A bacterial fermentation that sometimes occurs in new wines after the primary yeast fermentation. Malolactic, or secondary, fermentation changes natural malic acid into lactic acid and CO_2.

MEDOC: A red wine district within the Bordeaux region of France.

MERISTEMATIC TISSUE: The growth tissue of a grapevine, located in the cambium, shoot tips, buds, root tips and flower. Meristematic tissue is composed of thin-walled, actively growing cells that form new cells by dividing.

MÉTHODE CHAMPENOISE: The traditional bottle-fermented method for producing sparkling wines, including hand riddling and disgorging.

MICROCLIMATE: The localized climate in a specific, small area as opposed to the overall climate of the larger, surrounding region. A microclimate can be very small, as to encompass a single vine, or can cover a whole vineyard of several acres or more. Microclimates can be caused by slope of the land, soil type and color, fog, exposure, wind and possibly many other factors.

MILDEW: A grapevine disease. It can be devastating but is usually controlled by dusting the vines with sulfur or spraying with organic fungicides.

MINERAL IONS: Electrically charged forms of minerals, usually occurring in solution in the soil moisture and available for takeup by roots.

MISSION: The first of California's line of wine grapes.

MUSCATEL: Wine made from muscat grapes, usually sweet and usually high in alcohol.

MUST: The liquid (mostly) portion of freshly crushed grapes (before fermentation). Includes pulp, skins, seeds, juice and bits of stem.

NOBLE ROT: A common name for *botrytis cinerea*, the famous fungus of more than a few fabulous dessert wines.

NODES: Slight enlargements occurring at more or less regular intervals along the length of vine shoots and canes. One leaf develops at each of these nodes, and a new bud forms in the axil at the node also.

NOSE: The odor of a wine, including aroma and bouquet.

OAKY: A term used to describe the oak flavor in a wine.

OIDIUM: French word for the fungal vine disease "powdery mildew."

OPEN-TOP TANKS: Wine tanks without permanent covers, used only for red wine fermentation.

OVERCROPPED: A vine that carries more crop than it can reasonably ripen. Vines that aren't pruned drastically enough tend to set too much crop. Wine produced from fruit of an overcropped vine is always poorer in quality than if the crop were normal size.

OVERCROPPING: The act of allowing vines to set too much fruit (usually by pruning too lightly in winter).

OXIDATION: An adverse change in wine flavor, stability and/or color caused by excessive exposure to air.

LOUIS PASTEUR: The father of modern winemaking and pasteurized milk. He correctly identified yeasts as the causative organisms for fermentation and developed a heat process (pasteurization) for stabilizing wine, milk and other liquid foods from spoilage.

PETILLANT: A term describing a wine that is noticeably sparkling or bubbly with CO_2 but is less carbonated than champagne.

PETIOLE: The stem that attaches a leaf to its main branch or shoot.

pH: A term that defines the acidity of juice and wine. It represents the concentration of hydrogen ions in a solution.

PHOTOSYNTHESIS: The process in which sunlight is used by the green tissue of plants to convert CO_2 into sugars.

GLOSSARY

PHYLLOXERA: A microscopic aphid that lives on vine roots by sucking their juice. The aphid kills European wine varieties, but native American vine roots are resistant.

PINOT (PEE-noh): A family of grape varieties, notably Pinot Blanc, Pinot Gris and Pinot Noir (NWAHR).

POLYPHENOLS: A chemical class of compounds that occur naturally in wine, giving it an astringent, bitter or mouth-drying taste sensation. Tannins and grape skin pigments are two prominent classes of polyphenols.

POMACE: The solid residue (primarily skins, seeds and stems) left over after the juice is pressed out of the must.

PORT: Any of the rich, sweet, alcoholic and full-bodied wines from the Oporto region of Portugal. Other countries also use the term for wines of similar type, but the original name is Portuguese.

POTASSIUM CARBONATE: A chemical to lower the amount of total acid in wine. Used during winemaking.

POTASSIUM METABISULPHITE: A source of sulphur dioxide used during the winemaking process to inhibit wild yeast growth.

POTASSIUM SORBATE: Used during winemaking, this chemical halts yeast reproduction, thus preventing renewed fermentation.

POWDERY MILDEW: A fungal disease of grapevines that, unlike most fungal diseases, thrives in dry climates.

PRECIPITATION: The sudden formation of solids within a solution, as happens in the fining of wines. The solids normally settle to the bottom as a sludge within a few hours or days and can be easily removed by filtration, centrifuging or simply racking.

PRESS: The act of squeezing the last remaining drops of juice or wine from pomace. Also, the machinery used to do such a thing.

PRESS JUICE: The juice obtained not by draining but by pressing fresh pomace. It is usually far more tannic (often bitter) than drained or lightly pressed (free run) juice.

PRESS WINE: Wine obtained by pressing newly fermented red wine from spent pomace. It is invariably more tannic than free run wine.

PROOF: A scale for measuring and expressing the alcohol content of liquids. The proof of a liquor is twice its alcohol content, i.e., 80 proof = 40 percent alcohol. Since wine is always much lower in alcohol than the range commonly used for proof, the term has no use in wine production or on wine labels.

PRUNING: The act of cutting off various parts of grapevines, usually in winter when the vines are dormant. Pruning develops the shapes of vines when they are young and controls the growth, fruit quantity and quality of producing vines.

PUMPING OVER: The act of pumping wine out from a bottom valve of a fermenting tank up onto the top of the fermenting mass in order to keep the solid "cap" of skins wet. This is necessary during fermentation of red wine in order to achieve complete extraction of color and flavor from the skins.

PUNCHING DOWN: The act of pushing the cap down into the fermenting liquid to wet it and facilitate color and flavor extraction. This is the traditional method, but it can only be used for small tanks. Larger tanks are pumped over.

PUNT: The concave indentation in the bottom of certain wine bottles, especially those containing sparkling wine. Its main purpose is to collect crystals or sediment (this only works if the bottle is standing upright) so that the wine may be decanted easily.

PUPITRE: French name for the hinged, wooden A-frame rack used for riddling champagne bottles prior to disgorging.

RACHIS: The skeleton of branched stems that gives a bunch or cluster its shape.

RACKING: Decanting clear juice or wine from above the sediment in a tank. This is the easiest method for getting rid of solids that have settled to the bottom in a tank.

REDUCED: A term describing a state that is the chemical opposite of oxidized. In wine, the reduced state is usually recognized by the smell of rotten eggs (hydrogen sulfide, or H_2S).

RESIDUAL SUGAR: A term commonly used in wine analysis referring to the content of unfermented sugar in a wine already bottled.

RESPIRATION: The process in which plants produce energy, water and CO_2 by the interaction of oxygen and sugars.

RHINE: A famous wine river in Germany, as well as the name given to all German wines produced from vineyards near the Rhine River.

RHONE: A major river in southeastern France, flowing from Switzerland to the Mediterranean, as well as the name given to the wines produced from vineyards along the river.

RIDDLING: The process that causes the yeast sediment in champagne bottles to settle into the neck so that it can be easily removed.

ROSÉ: French word for pink wine, now commonly used all over the world.

SACK: The sixteenth-century name for sherry wine.

SAPWOOD: The outer portion of woody (xylem) tissue, located just inside the cambium and just outside the heartwood. Sapwood forms the primary highway for transmission of water and minerals from the roots up through the vine.

SCHLOSS: The German word for castle; on a wine label, it is equivalent to the French word "chateau."

SCION: The above-ground portion of a grafted vine.

SCUPPERNONG: One of the two major classes of native American grapes.

SEC: French term meaning "dry." However, on champagne labels it means that the wine is sweet.

SECONDARY FERMENTATION: Fermentation that happens after the primary (yeast) fermentation has been completed. Malolactic is a secondary fermentation that occurs in most red, and some white, still wines. Another secondary is the yeast fermentation, which changes still wine into sparkling wine.

SEKT: German word for sparkling wine.

SHATTER: A term used to describe berries that fall from the bunch quite easily.

SHOOT: The elongating, green, growing vine stem that holds leaves, tendrils, flower or fruit clusters and developing buds.

SHOT BERRIES: A few small, seedless grapes found in an otherwise normal bunch of wine grapes.

SOAVE: A blended white wine that is produced in northern Italy.

SOFT: A term for the taste of a wine that is low in acidity, flavor and body and tastes somewhat sweet.

SOUR: The taste sensation of acid. Not to be confused with bitter, which is the taste of some tannins.

SPAETLESE: The German word meaning "late harvest." These wines are usually sweet and high in quality.

SPICY: 1. A tasting term to describe a wine that tastes as if it had spices added during production. Gewurztraminer is the wine variety that is most often referred to as spicy. 2. Smell or taste sensation reminiscent of spices. The Gewurztraminer flavor is naturally spicy, especially when grown in cool climates.

SPUMANTE: The Italian word for sparkling wine. Equivalent to sekt in German.

SPUR: A shortened stub of cane, usually formed by pruning the cane to a length of only two to four nodes (buds). Spurs are obvious in the spring, after pruning but before new growth begins.

STABILIZATION: Any treatment or process that makes a wine stable, i.e., unlikely to suffer physical, chemical or microbial change.

STEMS: The rachis, or skeletal remains, of a grape bunch or cluster after the grapes have been removed.

STIGMA: The female (pollen-accepting) part of the grape flower.

STILL WINE: Wine that is not sparkling, i.e., does not contain significant carbon dioxide in solution.

STOMATA: The tiny openings on the undersides of grape leaves that control transpiration.

STUCK FERMENTATION: A fermentation that stops prematurely and refuses to start up again even though fermentable sugar still remains in the liquid.

SUGARING: Called "chaptalization" in France and most other countries, sugaring is the addition of common sugar to fermenting grape juice or must for the purpose of raising the eventual alcohol content in the wine. Illegal in some states, sugaring is usually needed only in very cool climates (or very cool vintages) in which the fruit fails to achieve full ripeness naturally.

SULFITE: The dissolved form of sulfur dioxide.

SULFUR DIOXIDE: A pungent gas used in wine to inhibit wild yeast growth, to protect wine from air oxidation and to inhibit browning in juice and wine.

SUR LIES: A French term meaning that the wine was held in contact with yeast lees longer than usual in aging and processing. The result is often a wine with a pleasant yeastiness and more complexity (though sometimes oxidized and bacterial) than ordinary wines.

SWEET POMACE: The solid grape residue after the juice is drained off but prior to fermentation. Primarily composed of skins, stems and seeds.

TABLE WINE: A legally defined category of wine that includes all wines with lower than 14 percent alcohol content.

TANNIN: A natural polyphenolic material that has a bitter or astringent taste, making the mouth pucker. Tannin in wine comes from grape skins, stems, seeds and from wood contact during barrel aging.

TART: Acidic (used as a pleasant descriptor in wine tasting).

TARTARIC ACID: The most prominent natural acid of grapes, juice or wine.

TENDRILS: String-like, coiling growth from nodes of grape shoots that support vines by curling around objects.

TERROIR: Terrain (loosely translated), used in the special sense of "place," which includes localized climate, soil type, drainage, wind direction, humidity and all the other attributes that combine to make one location different from another.

THIEF: A type of pipette used for sampling wine from the top of a tank.

THIN: A term used in sensory evaluation referring to a wine that lacks body, viscosity, alcohol or sugar.

TITRATABLE ACIDITY: The measure of total acid in must or wine, which is expressed as its tartaric acid content.

TOPPING: The act of filling a barrel or tank to the very top with liquid, usually wine of the same type and vintage.

TRAINING: The act of guiding, pruning and attaching a grapevine to a trellis.

TRANSLOCATION: The process in which nutrients are moved through the grapevine.

TRANSPIRATION: Loss of moisture from a vine by evaporation through the leaves.

TRELLIS: The structure of posts and wires that supports a grapevine.

TROCKENBEERENAUSLESE: The highest category of sweet dessert wine produced in Germany. Meaning "dry berry selection," it indicates that the raisined berries are individually picked to ensure that only fully raisin-dried grapes are used for the wine.

TRONCAIS: The name of a category of French oak shipped from the Troncais region.

TRUNK: The main, vertical body of a grapevine that supports all the top growth.

ULLAGE: The empty space above the liquid in a wine bottle, barrel or tank. Too much ullage can lead to unwanted aerobic bacteria growing on the surface of the wine. This can be avoided by topping.

VARIETAL: A wine produced primarily from a single grape variety and so labeled.

VERAISON: The midway point in berry development, when they change from green to purple (in red grapes) or green to lighter green (in white grapes) and become soft.

VERMOUTH: A fortified wine, red or white, that has been flavored by the addition of various herbs and barks (originally wormwood). Vermouth is used primarily as an aperitif.

VIDAL: A French-American hybrid grape. Also known as Vidal Blanc.

VIGNERON: A common French word for wine grower or winemaker.

VIGNOBLE: A common French word for wine growing.

VIGNOLES: A French/American hybrid grape.

VINICULTURE: The science of growing grapes.

VINIFERA: See vitis vinifera.

VINTAGE: A term referring to the crop of a given year.

VIOGNIER: A v. vinfera species of grape.

YEAST: A fungus that feeds on the sugar in the grape juice, converting it into alcohol, carbon dioxide and flavor compounds.

ZYMURGY: The science of fermentation.

Works Cited

Adams, Leon D. *The Wines of America*. New York: McGraw-Hill Book Company, 1978.

Adlum, John. *A Memoir on the Cultivation of the Vine in America, and the Best Mode of Making Wine*. Washington, D.C.: Davis and Force, 1823.

Atticks, Kevin. *Discovering Maryland Wineries*. Baltimore, MD: Resonant Publishing, 1999.

Burnaby, Andrew. *Travels through the Middle Settlements in North America*. London, 1798, 55.

Cattell, Hudson. "Remembering the Contributions of Philip Wagner." *American Wine Society Journal* (Spring 1997): 12–16.

Cattell, Hudson, and Linda Jones McKee. "Dry Table Wines for the East— The Roles of Fournier, Frank, Hosteter and Wagner." *American Wine Society Journal* 24, no. 1 (1992): 4–7.

Dresser, Michael. "Md. Wine Forecast: Partly Sunny." *Baltimore Sun*, September 30, 1990.

Eckrich, Ron. "Md. Wines Go Unnoticed Before Their Time; Vintners Try Squeezing Recognition, Promotion of Their Product from State." *Washington Post,* June 8, 1989.

Green, Andrew A. "Regents Condemn Madel Lobbying." *Baltimore Sun,* May 13, 2006.

Herbemont, Nicholas. "Letter to Edward Stabler on Wine-Making," September 9, 1829.

Hiaring, Philip. "Wines & Vines Takes a Historical/Viticultural Tour of Maryland Wine Country." *Wines & Vines* 8 (1974): 24–27.

Hill, Michael. "Maryland Wines: Rich Cabernets Hold Promise of Good Years." *Evening Sun,* September 25, 185.

Lewes, Walker H.H. "The Battle of Franklin Farms." N.p., 1924.

Liebmann, George W., ed. *Prohibition in Maryland: A Collection of Documents.* Baltimore, MD: Calvert Institute for Policy Research, 2011.

Lukacs, Paul. *American Vintage: The Rise of American Wine.* Boston: Houghton Mifflin Company, 2000.

Lyons, Sheridan. "Carroll Winegrower to Report of 'Test-Tube' Grapes." *Carroll County Bureau of the Sun,* April 1985.

Maryland State Session Laws. Vol. 540, Chapter 90. 1828, 1829.

———. Vol. 593, Chapter 268. 1841.

"Maryland Wine: The Next Vintage." A report by the Maryland Wine and Grape Advisory Committee to Maryland Secretary of Agriculture Lewis R. Riley and Maryland Governor Robert L Ehrlich. 2005.

McGrew, J.R. "A Brief History of Winemaking in Maryland." Paper presented at the Symposium on Heritage of Agriculture in Maryland 1776–1976, Associates of the National Agricultural Library, Beltsville, MD.

Works Cited

Millemann, Michael, comment on the constitutionality of Maryland Senate Bill 812. February 23, 2006.

Mowbray, G.H. "Philip Marshall Wagner: 1904–1996." Obituary. *American Wine Society Journal* (1997): 35.

Naylor, Dick. "Small Eastern Wineries Feel the Market Pinch." *Wines & Vines* (1991).

Pinney, Thomas. *A History of Wine in America: From Prohibition to the Present.* Berkeley: University of California Press, 2005.

Prial, Frank J. "Philip M. Wagner, 92, Wine Maker Who Introduced Hybrids." *New York Times,* January 3, 1997.

Pursglove, David. "Grape in the Glass, Not Region on the Label Is What Counts." *Washington Times*, May 22, 1984.

Rodgers, Marion Elizabeth. "Mencken, Ritchie and Prohibition." N.p., 2011.

Russell, Jim. "A Chronological History of the MGGA Merit Awards." *Maryland Grapevine* (Spring 2004): 7.

Shields, David S., ed. *Pioneering American Wines: Writings of Nicholas Herbemont, Master Viticulturist.* Athens, GA, 2009.

Silverman, Sharon H. "The Vine Art of Maryland Winemaking." *Maryland Magazine* (Fall 1993).

Swift, Carolyn. "St. Michaels Winery Brings Life to Local Grape Growers' Vision." *Star Democrat,* January 23, 2011.

Van Dyke, Ed. "Philip Wagner at Boordy Nursery." *American Wine Society Journal* 21, no. 4 (1989): 110–12.

Wagner, Philip M. *American Wines and How to Make Them.* New York: Alfred A. Knopf, Inc., 1936.

"'We Did It Because It Was Fun.' An Interview with Philip M. Wagner." *Maryland Grapevine* (Winter 1996): 13.

"'We Loved the Whole Idea of Wine.' An Interview with G. Hamilton Mowbray." *Maryland Grapevine* (Spring 1997): 11.

Williamson, Elizabeth. "A Growing Taste for the Fruits of their Labor." *Washington Post*, April 7, 2005, HO12.

Wolf, Judy. "MGGA—The Beginnings: Reprinted from the first issue of the *Maryland Grapevine*, 1981." *Maryland Grapevine* (Fall 2001): 6.

www.maryland.gov

www.marylandwine.com

Zibart, Eve. "Md. Toasts a Ripening New Industry." *Washington Post*, September 19, 1985.

About the Author

Regina Mc Carthy has been working with the local wine industry since 2009, specifically as the marketing coordinator for the Maryland Wineries Association. A native Marylander, she loves the local food and wine culture of the Free State and has a passion for both cooking and entertaining. Regina graduated from Towson University with her degree in mass communication with a focus on public relations. She has written articles for various publications, including *Reader's Digest: North American Wine Routes: A Travel Guide of Wines and Vines from Napa to Nova Scotia*. Working with the owners and staff of all the Maryland wineries on a day-to-day basis has not only prepared her for the documentation of this local history but also adds to her quality of life. Regina enjoys the many characters and the varied personalities who make up the local wine scene and appreciates their dedication to the land and hope for the future of the Maryland wine industry.

Tasting Notes

Take notes as you visit wineries and taste their unique vintages. Remember aromas, nuances, flavors and finishes. What meal would this wine complement?

TASTING NOTES

Visit us at
www.historypress.net

www.ingramcontent.com/pod-product-compliance
Lightning Source LLC
Chambersburg PA
CBHW070343100426
42812CB00005B/1411